First World War
and Army of Occupation
War Diary
France, Belgium and Germany

51 DIVISION
Headquarters, Branches and Services
Royal Army Veterinary Corps
Assistant Director Veterinary Services
1 May 1915 - 28 February 1919

WO95/2853/2b

The Naval & Military Press Ltd
www.nmarchive.com
Published in association with The National Archives

Published by

The Naval & Military Press Ltd

Unit 10 Ridgewood Industrial Park,

Uckfield, East Sussex,

TN22 5QE England

Tel: +44 (0) 1825 749494

www.naval-military-press.com

www.nmarchive.com

This diary has been reprinted in facsimile from the original. Any imperfections are inevitably reproduced and the quality may fall short of modern type and cartographic standards.

© **Crown Copyright**
Images reproduced by permission of The National Archives, London, England, 2015.

Contents

Document type	Place/Title	Date From	Date To
Heading	WO95/2853 51 Div May 15-Feb 19		
Heading	51st Division Asst Dir Vety Services May 1915-Feb 1919		
Heading	51st Division Advs 51st Division Vol I		
War Diary	Bedford	01/05/1915	01/05/1915
War Diary	Boulogne	02/05/1915	02/05/1915
War Diary	Busnes	03/05/1915	11/05/1915
War Diary	Pradelles	14/05/1915	16/05/1915
War Diary	La Gorgue	18/05/1915	18/05/1915
War Diary	Locon	20/05/1915	26/06/1915
War Diary	Le Nouveau Monde	27/06/1915	25/07/1915
War Diary	Heilly	26/07/1915	31/07/1915
Heading	51st Division ADVS 51st Division Vol II August 15		
War Diary	Heilly Senlis	03/08/1915	31/08/1915
Heading	51st Division ADVS 51st Division Vol III Sept 15		
War Diary	Senlis	04/09/1915	26/09/1915
Heading	ADVS 51st Division Vol IV Oct 15		
War Diary	Senlis	01/10/1915	24/10/1915
Heading	ADVS 51st Division Nov Vol V		
War Diary	Senlis	01/11/1915	30/11/1915
Heading	ADVS 51st Div Dec Vol VI		
War Diary	Senlis	02/12/1915	01/01/1916
War Diary	Flesselles	02/01/1916	31/01/1916
Heading	ADVS 51 Div Feb Vol VII		
War Diary	Flesselles	01/02/1916	08/02/1916
War Diary	Daours	08/02/1916	29/02/1916
Heading	ADVS 51 Div Vol VIII		
War Diary	Flesselles	01/03/1916	15/03/1916
War Diary	Hermaville	15/03/1916	21/06/1916
Heading	War Diary Of ADVS 51st (H) Division From 1st July 1916 To 31st July 1916		
War Diary	Hermaville	01/07/1916	12/07/1916
War Diary	Villers Chatel	14/07/1916	15/07/1916
War Diary	Doullens	16/07/1916	16/07/1916
War Diary	Ribemont	20/07/1916	20/07/1916
War Diary	Fricourt (Camp W. Of)	21/07/1916	28/07/1916
Heading	War Diary ADVS 51st (Highland) Division 1st August 1916 To 31st August 1916 Volume 16		
War Diary	Fricourt	01/08/1916	04/08/1916
War Diary	Ribemont	06/08/1916	06/08/1916
War Diary	Pontremy	09/08/1916	11/08/1916
War Diary	Renescure	11/08/1916	17/08/1916
War Diary	Armentieres	18/08/1916	22/08/1916
War Diary	Steenwerck	24/08/1916	24/08/1916
Heading	War Diary 1st September To 30th September 1916 ADVS 51st Division		
War Diary	Steenwerck	01/09/1916	11/09/1916
War Diary	Fletre	25/09/1916	25/09/1916
War Diary	Doullens	30/09/1916	30/09/1916

Heading	War Diary ADVS 51st (Highland) Division From 1st October 1916 To 31st October 1916		
War Diary	Doullens	02/10/1916	23/10/1916
Heading	War Diary ADVS 51st (Highland) Division 1st November 1916 To 30th November 1916		
War Diary	Lealvillers	01/11/1916	24/11/1916
Heading	War Diary ADVS 51st (High) Division From 1st December 1916 To 31st December 1916		
War Diary	Bouzincourt	01/12/1916	10/12/1916
Heading	War Diary ADVS 51st (High) Division From 1st January 1917 To 31st January 1917		
War Diary	Bouzincourt	01/01/1917	13/01/1917
War Diary	Marieux	13/01/1917	13/01/1917
War Diary	Bernaville	14/01/1917	14/01/1917
War Diary	Buigny S Maclou	15/01/1917	31/01/1917
Heading	War Diary ADVS 51st (Highland) Division From 1st February 1917 To 28th February 1917		
War Diary	Buigny St. Maclou	01/02/1917	05/02/1917
War Diary	Brailly	06/02/1917	06/02/1917
War Diary	Frohen Le Grand	07/02/1917	07/02/1917
War Diary	Rollecourt	08/02/1917	08/02/1917
War Diary	Villers Chatel	09/02/1917	28/02/1917
Heading	War Diary ADVS 51st (Highland) Division From 1st March 1917 To 31st March 1917		
War Diary	Villers Chatel	01/03/1917	28/03/1917
Heading	War Diary ADVS 51st (Highland) Division From 1st April 1917 To 30th April 1917		
War Diary	Villers Chatel	01/04/1917	07/04/1917
War Diary	ACQ	07/04/1917	07/04/1917
War Diary	Hermaville	11/04/1917	11/04/1917
War Diary	ACQ	16/04/1917	16/04/1917
War Diary	Chelers	25/04/1917	30/04/1917
Heading	War Diary ADVS 51st (Highland) Division From 1st May 1917 To 31st May 1917		
War Diary	Chelers	01/05/1917	05/05/1917
War Diary	Hermaville	11/05/1917	11/05/1917
War Diary	Acq	13/05/1917	14/05/1917
War Diary	S. Nicholas	15/05/1917	21/05/1917
Heading	War Diary ADVS 51st (Highland) Division From 1st June 1917 To 30th June 1917		
War Diary	Roellecourt	01/06/1917	02/06/1917
War Diary	Permes	04/06/1917	04/06/1917
War Diary	Bomy	05/06/1917	05/06/1917
War Diary	Eperlecques	07/06/1917	20/06/1917
War Diary	Lederzeele	23/06/1917	30/06/1917
Heading	War Diary ADVS 51st (Highland) Division From 1st July 1917 To 31 July 1917 Vol 24		
War Diary	Leaderzeel	04/07/1917	08/07/1917
War Diary	Poperinghe	09/07/1917	31/07/1917
Heading	War Diary DADVS 51st (Highland) Division From 1st August 1917 To 31 August 1917 Vol 28		
War Diary	Poperinghe	01/08/1917	08/08/1917
War Diary	Watou	09/08/1917	18/08/1917
War Diary	Wourmhoudt	19/08/1917	28/08/1917
War Diary	Poperinghe	29/08/1917	31/08/1917

Heading	War Diary DADVS 51st (Highland) Division From 1st September 1917 To 30th September 1917 Vol XXIX		
War Diary	Poperinghe	01/09/1917	26/09/1917
War Diary	Wormhoudt	27/09/1917	30/09/1917
Heading	War Diary DADVS 51st (Highland) Division From 1st Oct 1917 To 31st Oct 1917 Vol XXX		
War Diary	Achut le Petit	01/10/1917	05/10/1917
War Diary	Boisleux Au Mont	06/10/1917	31/10/1917
Heading	War Diary DADVS 51st (Highland) Division From 1st November 1917 To 30th November 1917 Vol XXXI		
War Diary	Boisleux Au Mont	01/11/1917	02/11/1917
War Diary	Hermaville	03/11/1917	17/11/1917
War Diary	Ytres	18/11/1917	24/11/1917
War Diary	Henencourt	25/11/1917	26/11/1917
War Diary	Baizieux	27/11/1917	30/11/1917
Heading	War Diary Of D.A.D.V.S. 51st (Highland) Division From 1st To 31st December 1917		
War Diary	Baizieux	01/12/1917	02/12/1917
War Diary	Fremicourt	03/12/1917	31/12/1917
Heading	War Diary Of D.A.D.V.S. 51st Highland Division From 1st January 1918 To 31st January 1918		
War Diary	Fremicourt	01/01/1918	22/01/1918
War Diary	Achiet Le Petit	23/01/1918	31/01/1918
Heading	War Diary Of D.A.D.V.S. 51st (Highland) Division From 1st To 28th February 1918		
War Diary	Achiet Le Petit	01/02/1918	09/02/1918
War Diary	Fremicourt	09/02/1918	28/02/1918
Heading	War Diary Of D.A.D.V.S. 51st Division From 1st To 31st March 1918		
War Diary	Fremicourt	01/03/1918	21/03/1918
War Diary	Achiet Le Petit	22/03/1918	31/03/1918
Heading	War Diary Of D.A.D.V.S. 51st (H) Division For April 1918		
War Diary	Fouquieres	01/04/1918	06/04/1918
War Diary	Labeuvriere	06/04/1918	09/04/1918
War Diary	Ham	10/04/1918	22/04/1918
War Diary	Norrent Fontes	23/04/1918	30/04/1918
Heading	War Diary Of D.A.D.V.S. 51st (H) Division From 1st To 31st May 1918		
War Diary	Noreuil Fontes	01/05/1918	06/05/1918
War Diary	Moroeuil	07/05/1918	31/05/1918
Heading	War Diary Of D.A.D.V.S. 51st (H) Division For June 1918		
War Diary	Moroeuil	01/06/1918	30/06/1918
Heading	War Diary Of D.A.D.V.S. 51st (H) Division For July 1918		
War Diary	Moroeuil	01/07/1918	17/07/1918
War Diary	Moussy	18/07/1918	31/07/1918
Heading	War Diary Of D.A.D.V.S. 51st (H) Division For August 1918		
War Diary	Moussy	01/08/1918	03/08/1918
War Diary	Pernes	04/08/1918	04/08/1918
War Diary	Billers Chatel	05/08/1918	16/08/1918
War Diary	Moroeuil	17/08/1918	27/08/1918
War Diary	Factory Camp	28/08/1918	31/08/1918

Heading	War Diary Of D.A.D.V.S. 51st (H) Division For September 1918		
War Diary	Moroeuil	01/09/1918	07/09/1918
War Diary	Victory Camp Ecurie	07/09/1918	14/09/1918
War Diary	Moroeuil	15/09/1918	25/09/1918
War Diary	Victory Camp Ecurie	26/09/1918	30/09/1918
Heading	War Diary Of D.A.D.V.S. 51st (H) Division For October 1918		
War Diary	Victory Camp Ecurie	01/10/1918	03/10/1918
War Diary	Victory Camp	03/10/1918	03/10/1918
War Diary	Chateau D'Acq	04/10/1918	08/10/1918
War Diary	Queant	09/10/1918	09/10/1918
War Diary	Bourlon	10/10/1918	10/10/1918
War Diary	Escaudoeuvres	11/10/1918	12/10/1918
War Diary	Naves	13/10/1918	20/10/1918
War Diary	Thun St Martin	21/10/1918	23/10/1918
War Diary	Pave De Valencienne	24/10/1918	31/10/1918
Heading	War Diary Of D.A.D.V.S. 51st (H) Div For November 1918		
War Diary	Iwuy	01/11/1918	30/11/1918
Heading	War Diary DADVS 51st (H) Division Dec 31st 1918		
War Diary	Iwuy	01/12/1918	31/12/1918
Heading	War Diary DADVS 51st Division For January 1919		
War Diary	Iwuy	01/01/1919	09/01/1919
War Diary	La Louviere	10/01/1919	31/01/1919
Heading	War Diary DADVS 51st (H) Division		
War Diary	La Louviere	01/02/1919	28/02/1919

WO95/2853
51 Div.
May '15 — Feb '19
Ast. Div. Vet. Services

(2)

51ST DIVISION

ASST DIR. VETY SERVICES
MAY 1915 - FEB 1919

121/6390

51st Division

ADVS. 61st Division

Vol I

WAR DIARY
or
INTELLIGENCE SUMMARY.
(Erase heading not required.)

Army Form C. 2118.

A.D.V.S.
67th Division

Instructions regarding War Diaries and Intelligence Summaries are contained in F. S. Regs., Part II. and the Staff Manual respectively. Title pages will be prepared in manuscript.

Place	Date	Hour	Summary of Events and Information	Remarks and references to Appendices
Bedford	May 2nd	2.40 p.m.	Left Bedford 2.40 p.m. – Embarked FOLKESTONE, reached BOULOGNE about 10 p.m. with Divisional Headquarters Staff.	
BOULOGNE	2nd			
	3rd	9 a.m.	Left for BUSNES 9 a.m. arrived about 9.10 p.m. Forwarded arrival report.	
BUSNES	3rd		D.D.V.S. 3rd Army called.	
	4th		Allotted Veterinary Officers to various areas, & attended all ranks here in.	
	6th		Mobile Veterinary Section arrived at BURQUETTE on night 5/6. Arrived BUSNES about 8.30 p.m. O/C.R. arranged billets for same in orchard & farm buildings.	
	8th		Conference of all Veterinary Officers. Instructions on general routine of work returned.	
	11th		17 horses evacuated. Asked for Keymes 67th mounted for to save wastage.	
	14th		Left BUSNES for PRADELLES arrived about 2.30 p.m. 15 horses evacuated.	
PRADELLES	15th		Visited as many units as possible. To see how animals had stood journey – Found much rather badly galled owing to their being soft & to fly new harness which in many of cases is much too large – Advised necessary alteration being made. The Rosin I showed was very satisfactory, carried a good bit of trouble to take on fat, edges sharp & cannot adjust yet & causing sores. Hope carnes be Keenes till to give one – Mules with collars ...	

Army Form C. 2118.

WAR DIARY
or
INTELLIGENCE SUMMARY.
(Erase heading not required.)

Instructions regarding War Diaries and Intelligence Summaries are contained in F. S. Regs., Part II. and the Staff Manual respectively. Title pages will be prepared in manuscript.

Place	Date	Hour	Summary of Events and Information	Remarks and references to Appendices
PRADELLES.	May 16th		D.D.V.S. 2nd Army called - now temporarily in La area. Evac. Sick Line 6 A.D.V.S. 9th D. West our general routine of work etc.	
La GORGUE	18		Left PRADELLES 6.15 S am. for La GORGUE arrived 1.45 am.	
			13 horses evacuated.	
LOCON	20		Left for LOCON arrived 4 pm.	
	21		Visits all units. Animals shewed much work and rest - much improved.	
			5 horses arrived.	
	24		15 horses evacuated. Arranged to inspect all Remount depot area ranges for D.O.s to ascertain same. Before writing home to this Line.	
	26		D.D.V.S. 1st Army called.	
	27		Found 3rd (A.V.W.) Sec R.F.A. horses T. be going back in condition, ascertained cause	
			The shortage from remount depot. Arranged special attention	
	28		Still having some difficulty in acquisition with the Rig store - made satisfactory provision with local forge.	
	29		18 horses evacuated.	

D M Griffiths
A.D.V.S. 2nd Army.

1577 Wt.W10791/1773 500,000 1/15 D. D. & L. A.D.S.S./Forms/C. 2118.

WAR DIARY
or
INTELLIGENCE SUMMARY.
(Erase heading not required.)

Army Form C. 2118.

D.M.S. 57 Div

Place	Date	Hour	Summary of Events and Information	Remarks and references to Appendices
LOCON	June 5		17 Horses evacuated	
	7		A party of 267 Remounts arrived	
			Issued arm'd charger to V. Officer	
	15		15 Horses evacuated	
	19		17 Horses evacuated	
	26		16 Horses evacuated	
Le Nouveau Monde	27		Left LOCON arrived Le NOUVEAU MONDE. Mobile Veterinary Section in a group field.	
	28		Visited units. Animals travelled well	
	30"		There is considerable difficulty in transport accommodation of M. Veterinary Section. The G.S. limbered wagons are not large enough, a hire is often a considerable amount of forage. To be moved to some which have been sent the section but which are not sufficiently big & the wagons which is desirable & kept. Have applied for exchange from G.S. limbered wagon for an G.S. wagon. It would be very big if a light float could be issued to Mobile Vet'y. Section in place of one wagon. It could then be used for floating horses on for transport purposes when the ordinary horse drawn transport could be saved if a float were received. Sand bag under present arrangements. This is impossible	

Conrad (illegible signature)
Colonel

Army Form C. 2118.

WAR DIARY
or
INTELLIGENCE SUMMARY.
(Erase heading not required.)

Instructions regarding War Diaries and Intelligence Summaries are contained in F. S. Regs., Part II. and the Staff Manual respectively. Title pages will be prepared in manuscript.

A.D.V.S. 57 D.V.

Place	Date	Hour	Summary of Events and Information	Remarks and references to Appendices
Nouveau Monde	July 1		Trenching Coy. R.E. attached.	
	4.		Forge getting busy.	
	5.		Received nose bag for dysenteric horses — girth mules. Seemed too deep were cut with curved awl ⊘ made the eye of the bottom of nose bag. Cut out a slit in bottom of bag slightly smaller than nose piece (this is our piece given over, then placed the cotton waste round the wire frame work on top, 6 kgs waste in rotation — tied canvas stitches over ventilation holes which were in front of nose bag. Submitted suggestion of improvement. Commstr. satisfactory. Return reported that a little had been received stating that reports were on the review complete ready made.	
	6.		13 Horses evacuated.	
	8.		Arranged for old Remounts to be taken over by M'Mic Veterinary Section by no means to have notified arrival arriving with regiment.	
	9.			
	10.		L.1 Bly on rest — and evaporated	
			Received authority for nine f/case — Seemed fine — Easy work now.	
	19.		17 Horses evacuated.	

1577 Wt.W10791/1773 500,000 1/15 D. D. & L. A.D.S.S./Forms/C. 2118.

Army Form C. 2118.

WAR DIARY
or
INTELLIGENCE SUMMARY.
(Erase heading not required.)

Instructions regarding War Diaries and Intelligence Summaries are contained in F. S. Regs., Part II. and the Staff Manual respectively. Title pages will be prepared in manuscript.

Place	Date	Hour	Summary of Events and Information	Remarks and references to Appendices
La Nouvelle MONDE	Sep 20		Lt Macdonald A.V.C. arrived to replace Lt Bryan temporarily	
	21		2nd D.S. 1st Army called inspected Corporals at H.V.S. in from town	
	22		Remounts arrived very poor.	
	24		Lame remounts - 37 horses evacuated.	
			Arranged for R. Officer to attend retaining of all animals arriving coming over.	
	25		Visited A.D.V.S. to see demonstration by Lt Hornby Q.V.C. re intra derma different method of vaccination.	
HEILLY	26		Left La Nouveau MONDE for HEILLY arrived about 3pm. Remained CORBIE Station all night re detraining - 4 a.m. went to Met. Court re same. Animals arriving well, no injuries at all.	
	27-30		4 horses evacuated.	
	31		L' Anderson Q.V.C. reported arrival with 83rd Bde R.F.A. which is now attached this division Together with 1 Battery, 82nd Bde, 1 Bde, 85th Bde, 532 Bty Bde, 75th & 78th Field Coys R.E. & 57th Field Ambulance.	

Ernest M. Griffiths
C.D. 57th Division

121/6801

51st Division

A.D.V.S. 51st Division
dated
August 15.

Army Form C. 2118

WAR DIARY
or
INTELLIGENCE SUMMARY.
(Erase heading not required.)

Instructions regarding War Diaries and Intelligence Summaries are contained in F. S. Regs., Part II. and the Staff Manual respectively. Title pages will be prepared in manuscript.

Place	Date	Hour	Summary of Events and Information	Remarks and references to Appendices
HEILLY	Aug 3		Visited SENLIS selected site for Mobile Veterinary Section.	
SENLIS	5		Left HEILLY for SENLIS - owing to scarcity of water Mobile Veterinary Section is at FRANVILLERS.	
	6		Forwarded War Diary for July.	
	7		Orders were received for Lt. Macdonald to return to Vety Hospital.	
	5-10		Visited units in this new area.	
	11		Inspected 86 Remounts.	
	15		Mobile Veterinary Section moved from FRANVILLERS to BAVELINCOURT.	
	23-30		Horse on trek.	
	31.		Visited units with D.D.V.S. 3rd Army. This has been a heavy month for the Veterinary Officers owing to the continual moves of the mule & large number of mules which have been attached to the Division	

Ernest Wm MacGregor
A.D.V.S. 57th D.

121/7083

51st Division

A.D.V.S. 51st Division

Vol III Sept 15

Army Form C. 2118.

WAR DIARY
or
INTELLIGENCE SUMMARY.
(Erase heading not required.)

Instructions regarding War Diaries and Intelligence Summaries are contained in F. S. Regs., Part II. and the Staff Manual respectively. Title pages will be prepared in manuscript.

Place	Date	Hour	Summary of Events and Information	Remarks and references to Appendices
SENLIS.	Sep/15		Forwarded War diary for August.	
	14"		Issued Store Return to units.	
	15"		Mobile Veterinary Sect 51st D.n changed its location to BAIZIEUX, much more central.	
	20"		1/3 Durham Field Coy R.E. arrived in an appalling state — 25% animals lost to be evacuated on account of this condition. Distributed Remounts.	
	26"		A lot of work has been done during the month selecting & preparing sites for horse shelters for the winter. I have considered it advisable to evacuate a large number of animals this month which I have considered would largely benefit by a rest & little nursing. By doing this it will make the division more efficient. The sequence of the animals evacuated will be easily regained.	

Lieut-Col. Gregg
A.D.V.S. 51st Division

1577 Wt.W10791/1773 500,000 1/15 D.D.&L. A.D.S.S./Forms/C. 2118.

A.D.V.S. 5th Division

Vol IV

Oct 15

Army Form C. 2118.

WAR DIARY
or
INTELLIGENCE SUMMARY.
(Erase heading not required.)

Place	Date	Hour	Summary of Events and Information	Remarks and references to Appendices
SERAI-IS	Sept.		Visited C.O.N.I.T. and demonstration of the Extra. Ammo papered number of elimination of horses.	
	2nd		Reported visits to C.O.N.I.T. and result of pattern test.	
	6th		Forwarded war diary for Sept.	
	14th		D.D.V.R. visited artillery horse lines – cast 29 horses – being of an unsuitable type for artillery work.	
	18th		Started divisional forge for the purpose of making new shoes out of old ones. Hope to turn out 40 pairs of strong shoes per diem.	
	22nd		Lt. Anncara A.V.C. received instructions to transfer to 28th Brno.	
	24th		Lt. Anncara A.V.C. left.	

Signed Mr. Perry Major.
O.I.V.C. 57th Divn.
3/11/15.

A.D.V.S. 518 Divn

No. 8
Vol. V

12/774

Confidential.

Army Form C. 2118.

WAR DIARY
or
INTELLIGENCE SUMMARY.

(Erase heading not required.)

Instructions regarding War Diaries and Intelligence Summaries are contained in F. S. Regs., Part II. and the Staff Manual respectively. Title pages will be prepared in manuscript.

Place	Date	Hour	Summary of Events and Information	Remarks and references to Appendices
SENLIS	Nov 1st	6.30	Nothing to report during the month.	

Ernest M Pope? Major
A.D.V.S. ? Division

Dec 2/15

A.D.v.S. 51st In.
———
Dec
———
Vol VI

Army Form C. 2118.

WAR DIARY
or
INTELLIGENCE SUMMARY.
(Erase heading not required.)

Place	Date	Hour	Summary of Events and Information	Remarks and references to Appendices
GENLIS	1915 Dec 2		Reported that a man said to be an Hospital had been found to be standard. Investigated above as instructed to it. Complaints apparently in loading	
	" 3		the men to shift this man belong as owing to the latest having been torn off in transit – funeral nothing to place on again.	
	" 4		Capt. Douglas received orders to turn division report at 2am hospital.	
	" 5		Commenced taking the animals of the division for standard by the Inoculative polyphered method.	
	" 8.		Forwarded War Diary for Nov.	
	" 26		First forage made 423 bales heavy shower since 9o'c" now cleared owing to suspending work. Many units on the move.	
	" 31		Testing of horses carried out no opportunistic mem – an artillery unit finished by 31."	

Samuel M. Guyseyer
A.D.V.S. 3rd Division

9-1-16

Army Form C. 2118.

WAR DIARY
or
INTELLIGENCE SUMMARY.
(Erase heading not required.)

Army Form C. 2118.

Vol 7

Place	Date	Hour	Summary of Events and Information	Remarks and references to Appendices
SENLIS.	Jany/16			
	1st		Innoculation of animals continued.	AppA
FLESSELLES.	2nd		Left SENLIS for FLESSELLES.	AppB
	3rd		Inspected new area.	AppC
	4th			AppD
	6–8th		Arranged for to continue visiting animals.	
			During continued inoculation duties, including attacks mini-	
			Corps of Army.	AppE
	9th		Forwarded War Diary for Dec.	AppF
	13th		Mass S.Ph. on dog. Diagnosis Rabies. – Reported same to DDVS.	AppG
	22nd		Lt. Burton A.V.C. relieving Lt. MacRaye in command of Mobile Vety Section.	AppH
	31st		Lectures to Officers of newly formed Mobile Vety Section on Horse management.	AppI

E.W. Ruppmann
ADVS 67th Divn.

51

aw v.s 51 Div
Feb
Vol VIII

WAR DIARY
or
INTELLIGENCE SUMMARY.
(Erase heading not required.)

Army Form C. 2118.

Instructions regarding War Diaries and Intelligence Summaries are contained in F. S. Regs., Part II. and the Staff Manual respectively. Title pages will be prepared in manuscript.

Place	Date	Hour	Summary of Events and Information	Remarks and references to Appendices
FLESSELLES	Feby/1/16	1-4 pm	Lectures daily to officers of the divison Cyc.	
		6.	Tournaments Cross Crazy for gang.	
		8-16	Proceeded to England on Leave.	
DAOURS.		8.	Division proceeded to DAOURS.	
		17.	Inspected nulls	
		23.	Snow fell & frosty weather.	
		25.	Heavy snow fall – Very bad travelling	
		29.	1/4 DAOURS for FLESSELLES.	

Edward M. Perry(?) Capt
A.D.S.S. 61st Divn
1/3/16

51

a&V.S. 51 Div

Vol XX / VIII

WAR DIARY
or
INTELLIGENCE SUMMARY
(Erase heading not required.)

Army Form C. 2118.

Place	Date	Hour	Summary of Events and Information	Remarks and references to Appendices
FLESSELLES	March/16.			
	1 to 6		Remained at FLESSELLES.	
	8th		Proceeded to BOZVAL. Weather during the period was very cold & frosty with occasional snow.	
	9th		Left for FREVENT remaining here until 12th.	
	12th		Left FREVENT for DUISAN — Weather improved — saw many times Army Horses affected with MANGE.	
	13th		Visited all villages in the area & interviewed respective Maires re location & obtaining & retaining of appliances with Mange. Some many sick horses — had them marked accordingly & obtained an order to Dirt R. Asies to the effect that no horses were to be put with copes.	
	14th		Left for HERMAVILLE	
	15th		Arranged for disinfection of new stables therein. Obtained 20 Blow Lamps had as stirrups which traits with this thoroughly & afterwards with strong disinfectant — D.Os to report when this had been carried out — All the wooden stalls in the area created by	

WAR DIARY
or
INTELLIGENCE SUMMARY

Army Form C. 2118.

Place	Date	Hour	Summary of Events and Information	Remarks and references to Appendices
HERMAVILLE	March 6/15		continued The French were found to be affected with MANGE. Obtained a fresh order issued that the Animals were to be put into shelter without permission D.A.D.V.S. This was an order I thought sanction even for certain sick animals which might require slight continuous treatment, but all shelter in the open kept. The 16" Heavy Battery arriving in this area, found 4 cases of mange in it. Nowhere has there been had mud worse. During the early part of the month the Division was continually on the move pursuing Von Kluck — the weather has been bad. Trying for the animals but generally speaking they have stood it well.	

Ernest M. Pitchford
A.D.V.S. 5ᵗʰ

Army Form C. 2118.

WAR DIARY
or
INTELLIGENCE SUMMARY.
(Erase heading not required.)

Place	Date	Hour	Summary of Events and Information	Remarks and references to Appendices
HERMAVILLE	April 1st 1916	6.30	Nothing to report.	

WAR DIARY
or
INTELLIGENCE SUMMARY.

Army Form C. 2118.

ADVS 51 Div Vol 10

Place	Date	Hour	Summary of Events and Information	Remarks and references to Appendices
HERMAVILLE	1916 May 17"		Had more trouble with Colic amongst H.Q. Animals, considered same due to Alfalfa Hay feeding. This made the third occurrence - Reported on same. Taking further connection. Ernest Sh— Pry/Major ADVS 51 Div	

Army Form C. 2118.

WAR DIARY
or
INTELLIGENCE SUMMARY.
(Erase heading not required.)

Army Form C. 2118.

ADV S 572

Vol 19

Place	Date	Hour	Summary of Events and Information	Remarks and references to Appendices
HERMAVILLE	1916 June 5	5ᵃ	2/7 F.S. inspected 253rd (Bde ?) T.F.Cᵒ	
		8ᵃ	Ditto inspected 258th " "	
		9ᵃ	Ditto inspected 256th " "	
		11ᵃ	1/6 Coroner of Capt Bryan A.V.C. as directed by A.D.V.S. for being absent without leave. Carried out.	
		12ᵃ	Received notice of arrival of Strainers amongst horses of 25th D.	
		13ᵃ	Arranged for the disruption of pus under charge W/Cpl H. Towers to suppls by 25th Div. veterinary Surgeon.	
		14ᵃ·/12ᵐ	Location statistics of all animals received from 25th D.: Leaving of 1503 animals which many have been in contact with these. Lt. Sugar went to R.V.S. showing some obstruction by W/Culpepper and others. The return of the Substances makes up to 3 weeks returns gave a negative result.	

Lewis Wm. Perry Major
A.D.V.S. 6? Dᵛ

CONFIDENTIAL
No. 3092A
HIGHLAND
DIVISION

Vol 12A

Confidential

War Diary

of

ADVS. 51st (H) Division.

From 1st July 1916 to 31st July 1916.

(Volume)

WAR DIARY
or
INTELLIGENCE SUMMARY.

(Erase heading not required.)

Army Form C. 2118.

CONFIDENTIAL
No J092 (A
HIGHLAND
DIVISION.

Place	Date	Hour	Summary of Events and Information	Remarks and references to Appendices
HERMAVILLE	1916 July 1st		Animals received from 25th Divn. Still continue to break out with mange.	Sgd.
	5"		Interview A.D.S. 60th D. Preparatory to handing over.	Sgd.
	7"		D.D.V.S. called.	Sgd.
	11"		D.D.V.S. called - inspected animals received as partial return from 25th Divn. none re-innoculated. no reaction.	Sgd.
	12"		Visits Jorskie Hunan with D.D.V.S. animals out.	Sgd.
VILLERS CHATEL	14"		WESTERMAVILLE - Lt. JOHNSON A.V.C. reports to replace Capt Dyson A.V.C. who goes to Etaples Hospital.	Sgd.
	15"		Left for DOULLENS.	Sgd.
DOULLENS	16"		Left for TRIBEAUCOURT.	Sgd.
TRIBEAUCOURT	19"		Left for TRISEMONT via FLESSELLES.	Sgd.
TRISEMONT	20"		Lt. DONNELLY A.V.C. reports to replace Capt MACKENZIE AVC. who goes to 13 ans Hospital.	Sgd.
FRICOURT (Camps W.P.)	27"		Left for FRICOURT (camps W.P.) During the moon anxious hour far the wall.	Sgd.
	28"		Arranges to have a new collecting station at Paines - found to answer well.	Sgd.
	28"		Attends conference at D.D.V.S. office	Sgd.

EwaTh. Sissy Major
A.D.V.S.
51st (H) Divn.

5.30 pm
10/8/16

CONFIDENTIAL
No 31(A)
HIGHLAND
DIVISION.

Vol 14

Diary

of

H.Q. 51st (Highland) Division.

1st August, 1916 to 31st August, 1916.

Volume 16.

CONFIDENTIAL Army Form C. 2118.
No 21 (A)
HIGHLAND DIVISION

WAR DIARY
or
INTELLIGENCE SUMMARY.
(Erase heading not required.)

Instructions regarding War Diaries and Intelligence Summaries are contained in F.S. Regs., Part II. and the Staff Manual respectively. Title pages will be prepared in manuscript.

Place	Date	Hour	Summary of Events and Information	Remarks and references to Appendices
FRICOURT	1916. August 3rd		The Rear Collecting Station at Ribemont has been found to be very satisfactory - M.R.P.S. can evacuate cases there & all cases which require re-action clear very quickly. Animals can be attended to at the Collecting Station. Numerous rehearsals Tr. prior to entraining.	Div.
	4th		Collecting Station, which if allowed to starve at Tr. M.P.S. for some hours would require fortnightly. Had a 5/7 journal in recent inspections of cont'd animals. Horses fr. vnits to Rr. high in many cases after Tr. move & continued hard work. A great many casualties being received. Only front worn horses. Two ones received.	Div. Fd.Q. St.Q. E.Q.p. C.Q.p. C.Q.p. St.Q. St.F.
RIBEMONT.	6th		left FRICOURT for RIBEMONT.	
PONT REMY.	9th		left RIBEMONT for PONT REMY.	
	10-11		Animals entraining at PONT REMY and LONG PRE.	
RENESCURE	1st		left PONT REMY for RENESCURE.	
	12th		Unloading of animals all came through well.	
	13th		D.D.V.S. 2nd Army called.	

Army Form C. 2118.

WAR DIARY
or
INTELLIGENCE SUMMARY.
(Erase heading not required.)

Instructions regarding War Diaries and Intelligence
Summaries are contained in F. S. Regs., Part II.
and the Staff Manual respectively. Title pages
will be prepared in manuscript.

Place	Date	Hour	Summary of Events and Information	Remarks and references to Appendices
RENESCURE	August 13-17		Visited A.D.S.S. 12th N.Z. Division re Taking over. Inspection during found animals and Harness well.	S.S.P.
ARMENTIERES	18.		Left RENESCURE for ARMENTIERES.	6 S.S.P.
"	22.		Inspection of all animals in 12 Division for mange commenced.	S.S.P.
STEENWERCK	24.		Left ARMENTIERES for STEENWERCK	S.S.P.

Edward Perry Major
A.D.S.S. 12th Division

Confidential.

Vol 15

CONFIDENTIAL.
No 21/A.
HIGHLAND DIVISION.

Diary.

1st an September to 30th September, 1916.

A. L. G. S. 51st Division.

Confidential.

Army Form C. 2118.

WAR DIARY
or
INTELLIGENCE SUMMARY.
(Erase heading not required.)

Instructions regarding War Diaries and Intelligence Summaries are contained in F. S. Regs., Part II and the Staff Manual respectively. Title pages will be prepared in manuscript.

Place	Date	Hour	Summary of Events and Information	Remarks and references to Appendices
STEENWERCK.	1916 Sep Cont.		During the week inspections have been carried out, generally with reference to the evacuation from one or two divisions or requiring a rest. A good many animals have been evacuated in this groups, and were evidence that, given a month's rest now, their animals would come or march good wepl animals to the winter.	
		11.ᵗʰ	Forty T. Remounts were received, evidently cast offs from other divisions very unsatisfactory - 20 of them have to be evacuated for various reasons.	
FLETRE.	25.ᵗʰ		Left STEENWERCK for FLETRE.	
DOULLENS.	30.ᵗʰ		Left FLETRE for DOULLENS.	

Edward Guy, Major
A.D.V.S. 51ˢᵗ (H) Division

2353 Wt. W3544/1454. 700,000 5/15 D. D. & L. A.D.S.S./Forms/C. 2118.

Confidential

War Diary Vol 16

51st (Highland) Division.

From 1st October 1916 to 31st October, 1916.

Army Form C. 2118.

WAR DIARY
or
INTELLIGENCE SUMMARY.
(Erase heading not required.)

Instructions regarding War Diaries and Intelligence Summaries are contained in F. S. Regs., Part II. and the Staff Manual respectively. Title pages will be prepared in manuscript.

Place	Date	Hour	Summary of Events and Information	Remarks and references to Appendices
DOULLENS	1916		Attended obtaining of muster at DOULLENS. Proceeded to BUS-LES-ARTOIS. On arrival visited roll inspecting resting places. Considerable difficulty in newmen of occupation of such & insufficient housing	
	2-10"			
	15"		Left Bn.S. W. ARTOIS for FEUVILLERS.	
	21"		Station side for advance Clearing Dressing station for N.U.S.	
	23"		James advanced dressing station. Very wet weather the Rain experienced in the month. It has been in a very bad state as there are no standings for the animals in this area - Convoy to evacuate have been constantly used especially to transport the Train arrivals - a great many artillery horses have had to be evacuated for debility - Have attention shown to their to recently a great now standing, new to make temps - horses got into a miserable state	

Ernest Mr. Scott Major
A.D.V.S. 9" D?

2353 Wt. W2544/1454 700,000 5/15 D. D. & L. A.D.S.S./Forms/C. 2118.

CONFIDENTIAL.
No 21/A
HIGHLAND DIVISION.

War Diary.

N. L. V. L. 51st (Highland) Division.

1st November 1916 to 30th November, 1916.

Army Form C. 2118.

WAR DIARY
or
INTELLIGENCE SUMMARY.
(Erase heading not required.)

Instructions regarding War Diaries and Intelligence Summaries are contained in F. S. Regs., Part II. and the Staff Manual respectively. Title pages will be prepared in manuscript.

Place	Date	Hour	Summary of Events and Information	Remarks and references to Appendices
LEALVILLERS.	1916 Nov 21st	10 a.m.	Very little to report. Animals have been in very trying time owing to bad weather, experience worth attention to. Stoneways material too rotten, but two general spare ring. Supt is fair condition - a few mules have been evacuated for glanders - Mules & Pickers up to mark - the latter, in consequence, from constant exercising, being chiefly Pickers, not the Mountain Types.	[initials]
	22nd			[initials]
	24th		Proceeded on leave - Capt Taylor acting in my places. Army Division to LA BOISELLE - OVILLERS - BOUZINCOURT.	[initials]

Ernest Th. Pilkington
A/V.S. 51st Y Division

CONFIDENTIAL
No 21(A)
HIGHLAND DIVISION.

Vol 78

War Diary

A. & Q. S., 51st (High.) Division.

From 1st December 1916 to 31st December 1916.

WAR DIARY
INTELLIGENCE SUMMARY

Army Form C. 2118.
CONFIDENTIAL
N° HIGHLAND DIVISION.

Place	Date	Hour	Summary of Events and Information	Remarks and references to Appendices
1916	Oct.			
BOUZINCOURT	3rd		Dr Lewis.	
		1-10	Rear Headquarters at BOUZINCOURT. Advanced Headquarters at USNA Hill. The whole of the A.D.S. has been experiencing heavy enemy shell fire, numbers of remonstrance necessary for the evacuation which have left this area. It is reviving conviction in his mind on my part on account of the mud surrounding the tongue. I would impress having been drowned. I am convinced the warning forces in to carry for very great majority of the General Field.	
			The two teams a big shortage of men in the artillery has consequently a certain amount of neglect of the animals which is quickly now in evidence. I regret to say with the Infantry transport animals when they are hard worked up to... time is sufficient... to keep the lines in good order. Serious overwork of the veterinary... the men is... months for the animals.	

Erneot Von Trothope
A.D.V.S. 51st D/v

CONFIDENTIAL.
No 21 (6)
HIGHLAND DIVISION.

Vol 19

War Diary

H.Q. 51st (High.) Division.

From 1st January, 1914. to 31st January, 1914.

Army Form C. 2118.

WAR DIARY
or
INTELLIGENCE SUMMARY.
(Erase heading not required.)

CONFIDENTIAL
No 21(?)
HIGHLAND DIVISION

Place	Date	Hour	Summary of Events and Information	Remarks and references to Appendices
BOUZINCOURT	1917 Jany 1st - 13th		During this period the various Units have been extremely busy. The extra work has meant Training perforce, in more than one respect, suffered. To be satisfactory training requires areas which are unencumbered by bodies not in training — but on ranges arranged I think the conditions of the Division have been more ventilated. The experience of the various Units has continued during the period of the training. There are continuous forms Coys Scouts + a large number of recruits from MARIEUX.	
MARIEUX BERNAVILLE	13th 14th		Lgr BOUZINCOURT for MARIEUX LGr MARIEUX for BERNAVILLE. Some ambulance work done at SARTON. Stoneham was subjected to an unsufficiently strong for the work thy have to do. Although they have a great advantage in having light is supper.	
BRIGNY St JANY.OR	15th	6.10.30"	Lgr BERNAVILLE for BRIGNY St MACLOU. Suspicion of mumps. Ambulances from coming Brigny will take a cold (ambulances for Bethany were operated on last days) move.	

WAR DIARY
INTELLIGENCE SUMMARY

Army Form C. 2118.

Place	Date	Hour	Summary of Events and Information	Remarks and references to Appendices
BULGNY ST MACLOU	1917 Jan 9th		Capt Burton A.V.C. returned from command of the Mobile Vety Section & was to 72/14 Veterinary Hospital. Capt F.T. Angle appointed to command of the Section.	
		16:30	Lectures to young officers in Animal Management have been given weekly for the subject personnel for their assistance. By the news of the movements the condition of the animals has greatly improved and not so much as used to arrive coming to the advanced position. Continuous frost with little snow has been experienced since Jany 14th	

Edwd Sm. Pish b Major
O. D. V. S. 6th D. |

CONFIDENTIAL.
No
HIGHLAND
DIVISION.

Vol 20

War Diary.

A. A. & Q. 51st (Highland) Division.

From 1st February, 1917 to 28th February, 1917.

Army Form C. 2118.

WAR DIARY
or
INTELLIGENCE SUMMARY.
(Erase heading not required.)

Instructions regarding War Diaries and Intelligence Summaries are contained in F.S. Regs., Part II. and the Staff Manual respectively. Title pages will be prepared in manuscript.

Place	Date	Hour	Summary of Events and Information	Remarks and references to Appendices
BRIENY ST MACLOU	1917 Feby 4		Lecture & instructions to Officers continued.	
	5"		Left BRIENY ST MACLOU for BRAILLY.	
BRAILLY	6"		Left BRAILLY for FROHEN le GRAND.	
FROHEN le GRAND	7"		Left FROHEN le GRAND for POLLECOURT.	
POLLECOURT	8"		Left POLLECOURT for VILLERS CHATEL.	
			During the whole of this move my cold weather experiences were in a very bad state for animals.	
VILLERS CHATEL	9" & 28"		The animals have shewn the effects of the march considerably. Above the 13" miles to march are in. Followed by rain which made the riding in a bad state. This was enhanced with the continual short rations & arrivals of the animals.	

Ernest M. Young Major
A.D.V.S. 51st Division

Vol. 21

War Diary.

A. D. M. S., 51st (Highland) Division.

From 1st March 1917 to 31st March 1917.

Army Form C. 2118.

WAR DIARY
or
INTELLIGENCE SUMMARY.
(Erase heading not required.)

Place	Date	Hour	Summary of Events and Information	Remarks and references to Appendices
VILLERS CHATEL	1917			
	June 1–8		Inspection of Units continued but owing to the centralised situation movement orders, am not able to report any improvements.	
	9–14		No special news.	
	22		Arranged & selected site in Brouay area for the advance Dressing Stn. for N.R.V. Station.	
	25		Special inspection of the Artillery Brigades. Farriery course showing effects of the hard work – horses going back in condition.	
	26		Arrived at the 34th, 84th & 315th Brigades Army Field Artillery. Inspections of above. They are in reserve also from Ostrely – came to Tournay area (C.Brie dressing S.) as noted.	
	27–28		No Br. emergency – to give special evacuation B.160 dressing mange cases – formed a special report & appreciation for Pomeroy. No arrivals of the 315th & 63rd Battery 34th Brigades on revision.	

Army Form C. 2118.

WAR DIARY
or
INTELLIGENCE SUMMARY.

(Erase heading not required.)

Instructions regarding War Diaries and Intelligence Summaries are contained in F. S. Regs., Part II. and the Staff Manual respectively. Title pages will be prepared in manuscript.

Place	Date	Hour	Summary of Events and Information	Remarks and references to Appendices
VILLERS CHATEL	1917		many horses having to be destroyed owing to exhaustion. The continued transport to work which has been a very severe one for some time — Given time an experienced man could I would the weather has been very trying indeed — I consider the average of the Divisional transport extraordinary and considering the conditions, notably horse wastage.	

Edward Shm Reid Major
A.D.V.S. 62nd D.n.

War Diary.

H. Q. U. S., 51st (Highland) Division.

From 1st April, 1914 to 30th April, 1914.

WAR DIARY or INTELLIGENCE SUMMARY

Army Form C. 2118.

Place	Date	Hour	Summary of Events and Information	Remarks and references to Appendices
VILLERS CHATEL	1917 April 1-7		Frequent inspections of the attached Army Field Artillery Brigades is continued. Many accidents are evacuated from the on account of debility.	
A.C.A.	8-15		Left VILLERS CHATEL for A.C.A.	
HERMAVILLE	16		Left A.C.A. for HERMAVILLE.	
A.C.A.	16-22		Left HERMAVILLE for A.C.A.	
CHELERS	23		Left A.C.A. for CHELERS.	

The weather up to the 21st has been especially trying for the animals. incessant cold frosty wind, with rain, this more or less continues until the general thorough of Remounts. On the 7th on the general condition. But 5 early evacuations the mortality from bronchitis debility has been to the Division. Little to nothing has changed particularly about the 26th 87th reinforce the animals have improved near Cely.

Two greyhound remounting horses have been arranged at S[T] NICHOLAS during the fighting. Red Cross morphine these renographs, as only a very few animals (15) were admitted the arrival there was also been gone on to their own units. There all the — in the ordinary way. Only on

WAR DIARY
or
INTELLIGENCE SUMMARY.
(Erase heading not required.)

Army Form C. 2118.

Place	Date	Hour	Summary of Events and Information	Remarks and references to Appendices
CHEERS	Apl 29/17		Men returning to the counting point. It is not used & every man is counted in the R.R.S. Sch. It was to afford to spare a N.C.O and 3 men at the counting point - Experience. I proposed to have the R.R.S. and German to surrounding posts at Brabham, return the R.R.S. on super closure of position - forward to wire or any I had arrived to see now coming when the army were not ready and the men were not doing hard work. Journeyed with the Divisions and visited the V.S. The animals are on the whole in very fair condition	

S. Stephen, Major
A.D.V.S. 67th Div

Vol 23

CONFIDENTIAL
No A
HIGHLAND DIVISION.

War Diary.

A. A. & Q. M. G. 51st (Highland) Division.

From 1st May 1917 to 31st May 1917.

Army Form C. 2118.

WAR DIARY
or
INTELLIGENCE SUMMARY.
(Erase heading not required.)

Place	Date	Hour	Summary of Events and Information	Remarks and references to Appendices
CHEERS	1917 May 1st		During this period the Division, with the exception of the Artillery, was out at rest. This gave a very good opportunity to improve its condition. The annual whole-meal ration drawing it.	A/c
	5th		1 N.C.O. & 2 men were sent on 6 day Information for Corps Hdqrs details. The visit bore the N.A.S. very short opening there anxiety.	A/c A/c
HERMAVILLE	11th		1/7 CHEERS for HERMAVILLE.	A/c
Q.C.A.	13th		1/7 HERMAVILLE for Q.C.A.	A/c
	14th		Divisional Arty. ordered to change to one Artillery Brigade. Can only answer the morning's outbreak to have the coolest with eight to arrive. This emigrated area — Enemy's attempts taken to eliminate 12 hours.	A/c
ST NICHOLAS	15th		1/7 Q.C.A. for ST NICHOLAS	A/c
	21st		Reports on the condition of the 2.36" Coy. 1st F.A. The C.Co.'s S.J.C. retired was very bad — means of cover inadequate. Every avenue throughout the Battalion.	
			Very fine weather has been experienced throughout the month so great improvement in the condition of the animals is evident.	A/c

Signed for Army hdqs
A.D.S. 57th Div.

CONFIDENTIAL
No 51/A
HIGHLAND DIVISION.

Vol 2/4

War Diary.

A.D.V.S. 51st (Highland) Division.

From 1st June 1917 to 30th June, 1917.

WAR DIARY
or
INTELLIGENCE SUMMARY
(Erase heading not required.)

Army Form C. 2118.

Place	Date	Hour	Summary of Events and Information	Remarks and references to Appendices
	June 1917			
Roellecourt	June 1st		Bar at St Nicholas	E.7.a.
	2nd		St Nicholas to Roellecourt	E.7.a.
Pernes	4th		Roellecourt to Pernes	E.7.a.
Bomy	5th		Pernes to Bomy	E.7.a.
Eperlecques	7th		Bomy to Eperlecques. Remained in this area until 23rd. All units took advantage of the rest. The majority of the horses were allowed to gorge in this hay improved considerably. The weather on the whole was excellent.	E.7.a.
	15th		The 1/8 Royal Duts. + 3 Field Coy R.E. left the Eperlecques area for the Zeperingle area.	E.7.a.
	19th		Divisional Horse Show was held at Eperlecques where a very suitable field was chosen for the event. There was a grand display by G.S. + Limber wagons etc in addition to various classes of horses which were exhibited in grand bloom. Unfortunately towards the close of the day the rain came down heavily thus spoiling the latter part of the programme.	E.7.a.

Army Form C. 2118.

WAR DIARY
or
INTELLIGENCE SUMMARY.
(Erase heading not required.)

Place	Date	Hour	Summary of Events and Information	Remarks and references to Appendices
Abeele	June 19th		Major Perry A.D.V.S. left the Division & proceeded to XV Corps as A.D.V.S. to that Corps.	P.P.Q.
"	20th		The 153rd Inf. Bde., 1 Field Ambulance + 1 Coy A.S.C. left MOULLE area for Poperinghe area.	P.P.Q.
Ledryzeele	23rd		Abeele gave to Ledryzeele. In this area the horses were again grazed where grazing was not available the horses were supplied with ample green forage.	P.P.Q.
"	24th		Arranged with the D.D.R 5th Army to visit Veterinary Hospital at Ouen for the purpose of selecting remounts for the Division. We selected about 50 which were not up to the Cavalry standard of remounts, as many were aged mares.	P.P.Q.
"	25th		Remounts collected from Veterinary Hospital at Ouen.	P.P.Q.
"	26th		Distribution of Remounts.	P.P.Q.
"	30th		Visited site of M.V.S. at Poperinghe which was taken over from 55th Division P.P.Q. the billets for the men are the I found this site an excellent one. horse standings etc. being very good.	

Army Form C. 2118.

WAR DIARY
or
INTELLIGENCE SUMMARY.
(Erase heading not required.)

Place	Date	Hour	Summary of Events and Information	Remarks and references to Appendices
Eecryche	June 29th		Many horses in the forward area wounded by shell fire.	See E.T.O.
"	30th		Lieut. to to Rem A.V.C. sent to the Poperinghe area to attend to the wounded E.T.A. with them.	

E.J. Angler Capt A.V.C.
for A.D.V.S. 51st Division

Confidential. Vol 25

CONFIDENTIAL
No 71(A)
HIGHLAND
DIVISION.

War Diary.

L. A. D. S., 51st (Highland) Division.

From 1st July, 1917 to 31st July, 1917.

Vol. 2 Y.

Original

WAR DIARY
or
INTELLIGENCE SUMMARY
(Erase heading not required.)

Army Form C. 2118.

51st (Highland) Division

Place	Date	Hour	Summary of Events and Information	Remarks and references to Appendices
Lanbrugge	4/7/17		Reports for duty as A.D.V.S. 51st (Highland) Division.	P.A.
"	5/7/17		Visited Div. H.Q. Arrivals. Div. Signal Coy & M.V.S. Condition of animals fair. 3 cases of mange in Signal Coy. Gave instructions to be sent to M.V.S. usual installation + disinfection adopted. Visited Capt Briggs (Corps MoDV2) home from fixing up mule details. Saw also for Supervisors mange.	P.A.
"	6/7/17		Visited Corps Supp. horses. 154 Infantry Bde.: 154 M.G. Coy., No 2 Coy A.S.C., 2/1 Field Ambulance.; Div. Signal Coy + Div. H.Q. Condition of animals satisfactory excepting M.G.C. which had several poor ones. One recovered was isolated for observation for skin disease.	
"	7/7/17		Journeyed by Car to Poperinghe for conference with A.D.V.S. 8th Corps. Visited Div. H.Q. on arrival + Signal Coy.	P.A.
"	8/7/17		Visited Div. Signals. Removed to Divisional Hd Qrs + Camp Poperinghe.	P.A.
Poperinghe	9/7/17		Visited H.Q. Div. M.M.P.; Div Signals (one case suspected mange). Visited Horse stps + S.A.C. (13 Echelon condition of animals very good; no I hock several poor animals. No 2 Section fair.	P.A.
"	10/7/17		Visited Div. Hd. Qrs. Signals. M.M.P. R.A. Visited 255 Bde M.H. (condition of animals	P.A.

Original

WAR DIARY
INTELLIGENCE SUMMARY

Army Form C. 2118.

51st (Highland) Division.

Place	Date	Hour	Summary of Events and Information	Remarks and references to Appendices
Proven	10/9/17 (contd) 11/9/17		Fair, might be much improved by filter (recommended etc.) Visited No Gr Dir MMP. tw Sqnds RE + RA.; Visited 1/2 (H) Field Ambulance (not very satisfactory). Visited MVS.	P.A.
"	12/9/17		Visited Sr.No 9r MMP. Sqnd Cy; RA; Visited with ADMS Corps, 255 F.A.Bde, consisting of accommodation for one care of mumps.; Visited 256 Bde R.F.A. several poor accmds + one case suspected mumps; Visited 510 M.C. 400, 401, 402 Field bys R.E. Three inspections were carried out along with ADMS Corps; Condition generally fair.	P.A.
"	13/9/17		Visited Sr. No. G. MMP. Sqnds R.A. + R.E.; Visited, with ADMS Corps, 58th & 59th Bdes R.F.A. Visited No 1, No 2 Cys A.S.C. 51st Div.; Visited MVS.	P.A. P.A.
"	14/9/17 15/9/17		Visited Gr.MID r Sqnds MMP. R.A + R.E. Visited Corps MODr, & Conferences with ADMS Visited "Q" Office re Clearance during station.; Visited 1/2 Royal Scots, 1/4 Seaforths condition of accmds fair. Visited 1/5 Argyll Sutherl. and Hylanders (evacuation pend.) 1/9 Royal Scots condn fair.; Inspected camps; 1/4 Seaforths Evacuation pend.; 1/5 Seaforth & Gorays, condn fair (improving); 1 Surfraet Pumps (present) 4 Seaforths Gordons, 1/4 J.M.Bty, 147 Bgde Siege Bde.; Visited 77 Bde R.F.A. + B4 condition good, one range case; B/54 condition good, 4 Gorays of Malaria, C/B, condition good. D/65, moved to Proven.	P.A.

Original

Army Form C. 2118.

WAR DIARY
or
INTELLIGENCE SUMMARY.

(Erase heading not required.)

51st (Highland) Division

Instructions regarding War Diaries and Intelligence Summaries are contained in F. S. Regs., Part II and the Staff Manual respectively. Title pages will be prepared in manuscript.

Place	Date	Hour	Summary of Events and Information	Remarks and references to Appendices
Ponoughe	10/7/17		Visited Div. H.Qrs. Signals R.A., R.E., M.M.P. Visited 11th F.A. Hos. Oration for Hughes to Rouen	P.a.
"	12/7/17		3 under observation. Visited 282 Bde A.A.S. oration for.	P.a.
"			Visited Div. H.Qr. Signals; R.A. R.E. M.M.P. Visited 11 F.A.Ho. with A.D.M. Corps. Visited 282 A.F.A. Bde.	P.a.
"	16/7/17		Visited Div. H.Qrs. R.A. R.E. Signals M.M.P. Visited + inspected annuals of 54th & 58th Bde.R.F.A.	P.a.
"	19/7/17		Visited Div.H.Qrs., R.A. R.E. Signals + M.M.P. Visited + inspected 255 Bde R.F.A. Conference with A.D.Os	P.a.
"	23/7/17		Arranged re Advanced dressing Station for advance dressing station.	
"			Visited Div. H.Q.rs. M.M.P. Signals R.A.R.E. Visited + inspected 256 Bde R.F.A. Visited out	P.a.
"	24/7/17		Visited Boys. H.Q. D.O. for Conference with A.D.Os. Visited H.Qrs. D.O. Signals A.M.P. R.A.	P.a.
"			Visited "B" Bty. 58th Bde. R.F.A. examined 6 animals, affects with fraspawing Imperfecta	
"	29/7/17		Visited Div. H.Q., R.A., M.M.P. Signal Coy. Visited Civilian animal effects with mange in field attaining "C" Bty 255 Bde R.F.A. Visited 232 Machine Gun Coy. Visited remounts of The Rallenos being two animals into their Remounts. Capt Connolly reported by Vet from home & evacuated to France.	P.a.

WAR DIARY

INTELLIGENCE SUMMARY. 57th (Highland) Division

Army Form C. 2118.

Place	Date	Hour	Summary of Events and Information	Remarks and references to Appendices
Pepenghem	23/7/17		Visited Div. HQrs. M.M.P. R.A. R.E. HQrs. & Div. Signals. Visited & inspected M.V.S. Visited 77th & 282nd A.T. Bdes. and A.D.V.S. Corps.	P.A.
"	24/7/17		Visited Div. HQrs. R.H: R.E. & Div. Signals. Visited & inspected 51st D.M.C. Visited M.V.S. & inspected same with A.D.V.S. & A.D.M.S. Corps.	P.A.
"	25/7/17		Visited Div. H.Q. R.A. R.E. & Div. Signals. Visited & inspected H.Q. 401 & 403 Btys. R.F.A. Capt. Buchan in acct. killed by shell.	P.A.
"	26/7/17		Visited Div. HQrs. R.A. R.E. M.M.P. & Div. Signals. Visited & inspected 152 Bde. R.F.A. Conference with D.D.	P.A.
"	27/7/17		Visited Div. HQ. A.Qm. R.A. R.E. M.M.P. & Div. Signals. Inspected 256 Bde. R.F.A. Visited M.V.S.	P.A.
"	28/7/17		Visited Div. HQ Divs. R.A. R.E: M.M.P. T.Signal bn. Visited Corps H.Qrs. & Conference with A.D.V.S. Visited M.V.S.	P.A.
"	29/7/17		Visited Div. H.Q.'s R.A. R.E. Div. Signals. M.M.P.	P.A.
"	30/7/17		Visited Div. HQrs. R.A. R.E. Div. Signals. M.M.P. Visited A.D.V.S. Corps H.Qrs.	P.A.
"	30/7/17		Visited three Divs. (A.D.V.S. Corps visits. Enemy attacked) 14 R.Orpe wary sp when allotted to 15 Corps. Visited M.V.S.	P.A.
"	31/7/17		Visited Div. H.Q. R.A. R.E. M.M.P. Signals. Visited M.V.S. & Advance Dressing Stn. Capt. Ellison act. reported for duty with 57th Division.	P.A.

L. Abercrombie Major A.V.S.
D.A.D.V.S. 57th Division

Vol 26

War Diary.

H.A.H.Q., 51st (Highland) Division.

From 1st August, 1914 to 31st August, 1914.

Vol. 28.

Original

Army Form C. 2118.

WAR DIARY
or
INTELLIGENCE SUMMARY

57th (Highland) Division

(Erase heading not required.)

Place	Date	Hour	Summary of Events and Information	Remarks and references to Appendices
Papenweg	1.8.17		Visited Divisional Troops. Visited 255th Bde R.F.A. Capt. L.B. Ellison A.V.C. reported for duty with 256th Bde R.F.A. Animals in good condition. O.R.S. not up to the standard. Issued reminder.	P.A.
"	2.8.17		Visited Headquarters Horse Lines. Visited 258th Bde R.F.A. Visited Advanced Dressing Station. Corps returned to Reigersvliet. Animals of 256th Bde R.F.A. in good condition.	P.A.
"	3.8.17		Visited 4th Montgomeryshire Horse Lines. Visited M.V.S. Conferences with D.D.S.	P.A.
"	4.8.17		Visited Div. Head Quarters Lines. Visited 152nd Infy Bde. Visited 152nd Bty Bde R.V.S. Mobile Corps.	P.A.
"			Mo.Qr. Conference with A.D.S. Animals of 152 Bde in fair condition.	P.A.
"	5.8.17		Visited Divl Hd Quarters lines. Visited Divisional Train. Visited 154th Infy Bde. Animals 20 injured in good condition ; Lost horses + Eleven mules killed by Bombs ; 20 injured.	P.A.
"	6.8.17		Visited Hd. Qr. Horse Lines ; Visited M.V.S. inspected animals for evacuation; Visited 31 + 1/3rd Field Ambulances. 1/3 animals not very satisfactory, several thin animals. 39 animals killed by Bombs - 17 R.F.A.Bde.	P.A.
"	7.8.17		Visited H.Qr. Horse Lines ; Visited Horse depot. Inspected M.V.S. inspected animals for evacuation ; Visited Advanced Dressing Station.	P.A.
"	8.8.17		A.D.V.S. Office moved to Watou. Veterinary ammunition of Field Artillery Bdes, Field Coys R.E., Div. Train, Mtd. Field Amb. Handed over to A.D.V.S. 11th Division.	P.A.

Army Form C. 2118.

WAR DIARY
or
INTELLIGENCE SUMMARY.   51st (Highland) Division
(Erase heading not required.)

Instructions regarding War Diaries and Intelligence Summaries are contained in F.S. Regs., Part II. and the Staff Manual respectively. Title pages will be prepared in manuscript.

Place	Date	Hour	Summary of Events and Information	Remarks and references to Appendices
Wardou	9.8.17		Visited HQ Dr Horse Lines; Visited 400, 401 & 404 Field Coys R.E. Animals only in fair condition. Visited 1/8 Royal Scots. Animals in poor condition. Conference with R.d.S.	P.A.
"	10.8.17		Visited S.O. Dr Horse Lines; Visited Corps H.Q. D.V.O. interviews with A.D.V.S. Corps & weekly out return.	P.A.
"	11.8.17		Visited H.Q.Q Wagon Lines; Visited Corps H.Q. D.V.O. Conference with A.D.V.S.; Visited D.A.D.V.S. 112 Division. Papersyth & return.	P.A.
"	12.8.17		Visited Bri H.Q. Ds Horse Lines. Visited Corps Mobile Vety Detachment at Proven re case of Strangles evacuated. Visited & inspected animals 152nd Bty. Bde.; Animals improving. Visited 1/2 (H) Field Ambulance. Animals in fair condition.	P.A.
"	13.8.17		Visited Bri H.Q. Dr Horse Lines. Visited & inspected animals of 153rd Bty. Bde. Animals in poor condition.	P.A.
"	14.8.17		Visited Bri H.Q.Dr Horse Lines. List over Veterinary Charges of 70th Infy Bde & 25 F Coy 23nd Dr Licom. Inspected animals of same units. Fair condition.	P.A.
"	15.8.17		Visited H.Q. D/O Dr. Horse Lines. Visited 372 Dr Train. Animals in very fair condition.	P.A.
"	16.8.17		Visited S.O./H.Q. Dr Horse Lines. Visited Proven Stn. inspected 95 Remounts.	P.A.
"	17.8.17		Visited Bri H.Q. Brigade Lines; Visited M.V.S. inspected animals for evacuation.	P.A.

WAR DIARY / INTELLIGENCE SUMMARY

Army Form C. 2118.

51st (Highland) Division

Place	Date	Hour	Summary of Events and Information	Remarks and references to Appendices
Lealvi.	9.6.17		Visited 152nd Inf. Bde. Animals inspected.	P.a.
	16.6.17		Visited Bde. HQ Or Stone Lines. Visited Corps HQ ADMS Conference with ADsVS	P.a.
			Moved ADVS Office to Wormhoudt - Visited Bde HQ Or Stone Lines	P.a.
Wormhoudt	19.6.17		Visited Bde HQ Or Stone Lines	
	20.6.17		Visited Div. HQ ADVS Horse Lines. Visited M.V.S. inspected animals for evacuation	
			" 70th Supp. Bde. HQ & Bty. 223rd Bde Siege V.a.(H) Field Ambulance	P.a.
			Animals in good condition.	P.a.
	21.6.17		Visited Bde HQ Or Stone Lines	P.a.
	22.5.17		Visited Bde HQ Or Stone Lines. Visited M.V.S. inspected animals for evacuation.	P.a.
	23.6.19		Visited Div. HQ Op Stone Lines; Visited 255th Bde R.F.A. Animals in fair condition	P.a.
	24.6.17		" " " Visited 157th Inf. Bde. Animals in good condition	P.a.
			Visited 232nd M.G.Coys. Animals in good condition. One case mange.	
	25.6.17		" Div HQ Op Stone Lines. Visited M.V.S. inspected animals for evacuation	P.a.
			" Div HQ Op Stone Lines.	P.a.
	26.6.17		Visited Corps HQ ADMS Conference with ADVS	P.a.
			Visited & inspected M.V.S.	

Army Form C. 2118.

WAR DIARY
or
INTELLIGENCE SUMMARY. 51st (Highland) Division
(Erase heading not required.)

Place	Date	Hour	Summary of Events and Information	Remarks and references to Appendices
Bertincourt	27/8/17		Visited Bde HQ & Horse Lines; Bde's & August 152nd Infy Bde. Animals in good condition; Visited 153 Infy. Bde. Animals in very poor condition	P.A.
"	28/8/17		Visited Bde HQ & Horse lines; Visited 154 Infy Bdes. Visited 1/2 (H) Field Amb. Animals improved. Visited 1/3 (H) Field Amb. Animals improving. Visited MVS. Inspected animals for evacuation; Visited Corps H.Q. Re conference with A.D.V.S. Returns sent in.	P.A.
Poperinghe	29/8/17		Visited Div HQ & Horse lines. DADVS office moved to Poperinghe.	P.A.
"	30/8/17		Visited + inspected 253rd Bde R.F.A. animals	P.A.
"	"		Not condition due to heavy work & climatic condition. Visited Div M.B. & Horse lines. Visited + inspected 2nd Dragoon Guards entire squadron. Animals in poor condition generally. 3 Debility cases + 1 Mange evacuated to MVS.	
"	31/8/17		Visited 152nd Infy Bde. Animals improving. A case of Glanders was found at Base H.Q. Majestic which has been evacuated from 7(B) M.V.S. from 1/7 H.T.B.Dep. concerned, all animals in units concerned have been traced to Ireland. No sickness reported.	P.A.

F. Allen Major A.V.C.
S.A.D.V.S. 51st (H) Division

War Diary.

H.Q. U.D. 51st (Highland) Division.

From 1st September, 1914 to 30th September, 1914.

Vol. XXIX

Original

Army Form C. 2118.

WAR DIARY
or
INTELLIGENCE SUMMARY. 51st (H) Division.
(Erase heading not required.)

Place	Date	Hour	Summary of Events and Information	Remarks and references to Appendices
Dieppe	1917 Sept 1		Visited Divisional Headquarters Horse Lines. Visited H.Q. Dn 18 Corps conference with A.D.V.S.; Visited 1/1 (H/1 M.V.S. inspected animals for evacuation.	P.U.
"	" 2		Visited Divisional H.Q. Dn Horse Lines; Visited 255-Bde R.F.A. inspected animals & Veterinary Equipment. Animals in fair condition. 2 Bdy - 6 poor animals; 1 case mange in "C" Bty.	P.U.
"	" 3		Visited Divisional Horse Lines; Visited & inspected 51st D.T.C. Animals in good condition generally. Visited 400, 401, 404 Field Coys R.E. with A.D.V.S. Strong & ADVS 18th Corps. Inspected animals 19 H.D. selected 6 to be replaced by L.D. Visited M.V.S. Inspected animals for evacuation. Visited Bde H.Q. Dn Horse Lines; Visited & inspected 153rd Wfy Bde. animals in poor condition. Visited 154 Wfy Bde. animals improving. Visited 282(?) M.G. Corps. Visited 3rd Traffic control squadron.	P.U.
"	" 4		Visited Divisional H.Q. Dn Horse Lines; Visited 1/149 M.V.S. inspected animals for evacuation. Visited 2/1 (H) Field Amb; animals in poor condition. Visited 2/3/H) Field Amb, animals in poor condition. (very much improved since last inspection). Visited 1/ Royal Scots (Pioneers) 17 animals killed by bomb, 12 were (Continued)	P.U.
"	" 5			

Original.

WAR DIARY
or
INTELLIGENCE SUMMARY. 372 (H) Burzew.

Army Form C. 2118.

Place	Date	Hour	Summary of Events and Information	Remarks and references to Appendices
Ramiyeh	1917 Sept 6 (contd)		were destroyed & 16 wounded, remaining animals in food condition (32 Ophthalmia cases) Visited Div. H.Q. Horse Lines. Visited King Edward's Horse Troops Batts., condition fair. Visited 3rd Traffic Control (Capt Lloyd in charge) & Capt Clover Squadron, condition fair. 404-401-403 Field Coys R.E. (care dehoum animals) Condition improving. Conference with E.O.	P.A.
"	7		Visited the H.Q. Div. Horse Lines. Visited Div. Train, inspected remounts before distribution.	P.A.
"	8		74 HMVS. Visited Div. Ophthalmia lines. Visited No. 2, 3 & 4 Coys. 5 Spt Div. Train. Condition good.	P.A.
"	9		Visited Div. Ophthalmia lines. Visited 3rd Traffic Control. Visited MVS. inspected animals for evacuation. Visited Corps H.Q. for conference with A.D.V.S. Visited Div. H.Q. Div Horse Lines. Visited 250/Bde R.H.A. condition unsatisfactory. 18 Cases Ophthalmia.	P.A.
"	10		Visited H.Q. Div. Horse Lines. Temporary hangers & 30 animals for Field boys to Div Eqpmts for special attention. Visited 256th Bde R.F.A. C.Bty pour condition. 17 prm. Ds Ophthalmia cases. 3 chaff cutters broken. Visited 3rd traffic control. Dannam in bad condition.	P.A.
"	11		Visited H.Q. Div. Horse Lines. Visited & inspected animals 376 Bde R.H.A. Condition	P.A.

(Continued)

Original.

Army Form C. 2118.

WAR DIARY
or
INTELLIGENCE SUMMARY.
(Erase heading not required.)

57th (1st) Division

Instructions regarding War Diaries and Intelligence
Summaries are contained in F. S. Regs., Part II.
and the Staff Manual respectively. Title pages
will be prepared in manuscript.

Place	Date	Hour	Summary of Events and Information	Remarks and references to Appendices
Poperinghe	1917 Sept 11th		Generally fine; 98 animals on line for transfer to Batteries; Visited 3rd Troops Control Operation (Capt Sloan)	P.A.
"	" 12		Visited HQ Q. Dr. Brit. Horse Lines; Visited Horse top.; Visited M.V.S. inspected animals for evacuation; Visited 405th, 406th, 408th Field Coys R.E. evacuation not satisfactory. HQ Coy has 10 thin animals; Visited 9th Royal Scots, several thin animals chiefly remounts; 11 cases of Yphthalmia; Visited 152nd Infy. Bde.; Capt Kirk R.V.C. reports for duty from No 12 Veterinary Hospital & attached to 258 Bde R.F.A. for duty.	
"	13		Visited Divl HQ Dr. Horse Lines; Visited M.V.S.; Visited 1/3rd (H) Field Amb., evacuation of animals good. Visited 2/1st (H) Field Amb. evacuation good. Conference with O.O's Brit. B.H.Q Brit. Horse Lines; Visited 258th Bde R.F.A. numerous thin animals to be evacuated; Visited 152nd Infy. Bde. all in good condition.	P.A.
"	14		Visited HQ G.H.Q Brit. Horse lines; Visited 152nd Infy. Bde. all in good condition. Visited 153 Infy. Bde. animals all in good condition.	P.A.
"	15		Visited HQ Div. Dr. Horse lines; Visited Corps HQ. Qn. Conference with ADVS.	P.A.
"	16		Visited Divl HQ Dr. Horse lines; Visited M.V.S. Visited 3rd Troops Control.	P.A.

WAR DIARY or INTELLIGENCE SUMMARY

Army Form C. 2118.

Original

57th (H) Division

Place	Date	Hour	Summary of Events and Information	Remarks and references to Appendices
Poperinghe	1917 Sept 17		Visited Div. H.Q. Horse Lines; Visited 3rd Traffic Control; Visited 158th Bfty. Bde. Visited Horse lines re 401st Field Coys. horse injured; Capt took over left for duty with 50th Division.	P.U.
"	18		Capt Anglin Rett. went on leave. Capt Taylor A/V.O. took command of 2/1(H) M.V.S. during Capt Anglin's absence; Visited M.V.S. inspected animals for evacuation; Visited 400th, 401st, 404th Field Coys. animals still unsatisfactory, average of sup; Visited 152nd Bfty. Bde.; Visited 153rd Bfty. Bde.; Visited Div. H.Q. Horse lines the animals from M.M.P. and 6 M.V.S. all sharp.	P.U.
"	19		Visited H.Q. Div. Div. Horse Lines; Visited 3rd Traffic Control; Visited Knights to 258th I.P. Bde., condition bad, evacuated 33 debility animals; Visited 255th H. Bde. evacuated 16 animals for Debility.	P.U. P.U.
"	20		Visited Div. H.Q. Div. Horse lines; Visited 152nd Bfty. Bde.; Visited 153rd Bfty. Bde.	P.U.
"	21		Visited Div. H.Q. Horse lines; Conference with D.D.S.; Visited 37 ton train inspected remounts for destination; Visited 1/6 Royal Scots. anne remounts in conversation; Visited Rambeckes Horses - inspected 123 remounts Visited 3rd Traffic Control, Normene Farm destroyed arrival injured by hrs.	P.U.

Army Form C. 2118.

WAR DIARY
or
INTELLIGENCE SUMMARY.

(Erase heading not required.)

51st (H) Division

Instructions regarding War Diaries and Intelligence Summaries are contained in F. S. Regs., Part II. and the Staff Manual respectively. Title pages will be prepared in manuscript.

Place	Date	Hour	Summary of Events and Information	Remarks and references to Appendices
Poperinghe	1917 Sept 22		Visited HQ Div Dis Horse Lines.; Visited 154th Infy Bde.; Visited 3rd Trophy Control (Capt Loye); 18th Corps HQ Div expenses with MDS.; Visited 400th, 401st 404th Field Coys.	P.A.
"	23		Visited Div HQ Div Horse Lines; Visited 153rd Infy Bde.; Visited 255th Infy Bde.; S.Bty still in her erection; Visited MVS. inspected arrivals for evacuation.	P.A.
"	24		Visited 2/5 Gordons Horse Lines. Visited 2/7 Trophy Control, Officers Mess Capt. Shaw, Squadron. Visited 268 RFA Bde. arrivals inspected. Visited 51st D.A.C.; arrivals in front condition.	P.A.
"	25		Visited HQ Div Dis Horse Line. LH DS Office moved to Woesten 97.	P.A.
"	26		Visited HQ Div Dis Horse Lines & MVS.; 255th & 256th FA Bde, 51st DAC RE. Received over to STADVS 11th Division for veterinary administration.	P.A.
Woesten	27		Visited HQ Bn Dis Horse Lines; Visited MVS.	P.A.
"	28		Visited HQ Div Divl Horse Lines. Visited Railhead Proven 3 to 6.30pm.	P.A.
"	29		during entrainment to arrivals. Moved to Ochust-la Pitt.	P.A.
"	30.		Visited Div HQ Div Horse Lines; Visited 152nd Infy Bde, Visited 154th Infy Bde; No 2 Cry ASC Visited MVS. Visited 400th, 401st 404th Field Coys.	P.A.

Percy Alwyn Mayer, Capt.
STADVS. 51st (H) Division

Vol 28

War Diary.

H.A. H.Q., 51st (Highland) Division.

From 1st October, 1917 to 31st October, 1917.

Vol. XXX.

WAR DIARY
or
INTELLIGENCE SUMMARY.   57 (Highland) Division

Army Form C. 2118.

Place	Date	Hour	Summary of Events and Information	Remarks and references to Appendices
Relief à Pekin	1917 Oct. 1		Visited Bde. HdQr. Horse Lines; visited 152 Infantry Bde; visited 232 M.G. Coys. "No 4 Coy. Bn. Train (57ths). Visited MVS; visited 400th 401st 404th Lurkey RF.	P.A. P.A.
	" 2		Visited Bde. HdQr. Horse Lines; visited 152 Infty Bde; 232 M.G.C.; 400th 401st 404th F.Cys. R.65. & MVS; Visited 1/2 (H) Field Amb.	
"	" 3		Visited Bde HdQr. Horse Lines; 152nd Infty Bde; 232 M.G.C.; MVS, visited Bertencourt, examined & inspected site for 1/1(H) MVS.	P.A.
"	" 4		Visited Bde HQ Qr. Horse Lines; visited HQ MVS, visited 1/2 (H) Field Amb. 153rd Infty Bde.	P.A.
"	" 5		A.D.M.S. Office moved to Bertencourt or Mont.	P.A. P.A.
	" 6		Visited Bde HdQr. Horse Lines; Visited 2/1 (H) Field Amb; visited & inspected arrivals 57 Stn train; Malleneis 11 arrivals 3 232 M.G.C. proceedings overseas	P.A.
Bertencourt au Mont	" 7		Visited Bde. HdQr. Horse Lines; MVS; visited VIth Corps HdQrs (Bulencourt) conference with A.D.M.S. (Col Fisher), Visited arrivals unfit Malleneis arrivals of 232nd M.G.C. (1 horse 10 mules)	
"	" 8		Visited Bde; HQ Qr. Horse Lines; visited 152nd 153rd 154th Infty Bdes.	P.A.
"	" 9		Visited 400th 401st 404th Field Cys R.65 (condition of arrivals unsatisfactory (contd)	P.A.

WAR DIARY
INTELLIGENCE SUMMARY

Army Form C. 2118.

57th (2nd) Division

Place	Date	Hour	Summary of Events and Information	Remarks and references to Appendices
Boulogne (06/4) an (and)	1917		*apparently no Hy. 12 arrivals b/the evacuated); visited 1/2 (H) Field Amb; arrivals in forts/tender; visited 9/(H) M.V.S.; visited 3rd Potato Park	P.A. P.A.
"	10		visited Div. HQ Div. Horse Lines; visited 91 (H) Field Amb; visited 57th Div. train visited Div. HQ Div. Horse Lines, visited 1/3 (H) Field Amb at Bercy en Artois	P.A.
"	11		1/6 Argyle & Sutherland Highland Horse Lines (arrivals in good condition) visited Div. HQ Div. Horse Lines; 400th 401st 404th & 676th R.Ss. Conference with N°6 Stencil R&s; visited 91 (H) Field Amb, 1512th 1513th & 1514th Hy Bties, 232 N.C.C.	P.A.
"	13		visited Div. HQ Div. Horse Lines; visited Corps H.Q. Gas experiment A.D.V.S.'s mules 1/3 (H) Field Amb at Gorey. visited M.V.S.	P.A.
"	14		visited Div. HQ Div. Horse Lines; visited 22nd Army Field Artillery Bde. Bries 152 & 154th Infy. Bdes. Capt. Taylor R.AVC. went on 10 days leave to England.	P.A.
"	15		visited Div. HQ Div. Horse Lines; visited 23rd Q.F.A. Bde + Amm. Col at Inchune 400th 401st 404th Field Coys R&s. (arrivals improved) visited 1/2 (H) Field Amb. visited 91 (H) Field Amb. + M.V.S.	P.A.
"	16		visited Div. HQ Div. Horse Lines; visited Fichens with A.D.V.S. Corps inspected (Cart)	P.A.

Original

WAR DIARY
or
INTELLIGENCE SUMMARY.
(Erase heading not required.)

Army Form C. 2118.

51st (H) Division

Place	Date	Hour	Summary of Events and Information	Remarks and references to Appendices
Bailleul au Mont	1917 Feb 14th & 15th		Inspected Nothing; Visited M.V.S.; Inspected 51st Divisional Train; Visited 51st Reserve Park A.S.C.; Visited 152nd, 153rd/154th Infantry Brigades Horse Lines	P.R.
"	Feb 17		Visited Div. M.G. Horse Lines; Visited 1/(H) M.V.S with A.D.V.S.; VI Corps; also 51st Divisional Train Inspected Horses; Visited 293rd Army F.A. Bde.; Visited 23rd Army Field Artillery Bde arrivals at Pernois; Visited 153rd, 152nd & 154th Bdy. Horse Lines; Visited 232nd M.G.C. &	P.R.
"	18		Visited Div. No Div Horse Lines; Visited 1/(H) M.V.S. Visited 51st Train Inspected Removals (animals much worn & in low condition); Visited 23rd Divisional Ammn. Col. "C" Bty.; Visited 50th Divisional Ammn Col (Organised with P.O.S.	P.R.
"	19		at Lichera Bde. 1/6 Argyle & Sutherlands.; Visited 293rd A.F.A. Bde along with A.D.V.S. 3rd Army & A.D.V.S. VII Corps (Condition of animals good); Visited 152nd + 154th Bty. Bdes.	P.R.
"	20		Visited Div. H.Q. Gp. Horse Lines; Visited VI Corps H.Q. Div. Conferences with A.D.V.S. Visited 1/3 (H) Field Amb. at Ervey; Visited Stables (2nd) A.F.A. Bde + Bde Ammn Col.; Visited 152nd Bty. Bde., 232 M.G.C. (continued)	P.R.

2353 Wt. W2544/1454 700,000 5/15 D. D. & L. A.D.S.S. Forms/C.2118.

Original

WAR DIARY
or
INTELLIGENCE SUMMARY.
(Erase heading not required.)

Army Form C. 2118.

57th (H) Division

Place	Date	Hour	Summary of Events and Information	Remarks and references to Appendices
Bois Carré (see map)	1917 Oct 20 (cont)		Visited No 1 Coy. 27th Reserve Park A.S.C.	P.U.
	21		" " H.Q. G.Horse Lines; Visited 400th, 401st, 404th Stud Coys R.E. (Animals much improved); Visited 1/2 (H) Field Amb (Animals in good condition)	P.U.
	22		Visited Bn HQ. G.Horse Lines; Visited 152nd, 153rd & 154th Infy Bdes 232nd MGC; Visited 1/2 (H) M.V.S.	P.U.
	23		Visited Bn HQ G.Horse Lines; Visited & inspected 256th H.A.Bde at Berthancourt (Animals generally in good condition; 24 cases Nostes dermatitis) Inspected 253rd H.A.Bde at Achiens (Animals in good condition generally) Inspected 517 Div Amm Col. at Louvencourt (Animals in good condition) Visited Bn HQ. G. Horse Lines; Visited 152nd, 153rd & 154th Infy Bdes.	P.U.
	24		Visited 23rd Army F.A.Bde	P.U.
	25		Visited Bn HQ G.Horse Lines; M.V.S. Visited Achiens, Berthancourt & Louvencourt inspected Animals of 255th, 251st Bdes R.H.A & 519th Div Amm Col. for evacuation.	P.U.
	26		Visited Bn HQ G.Horse Lines; Visited Achiens, Berthancourt & Louvencourt (cont)	P.U.

Army Form C. 2118.

Original

WAR DIARY
or
INTELLIGENCE SUMMARY. 57th (1st H) Division

(Erase heading not required.)

Instructions regarding War Diaries and Intelligence Summaries are contained in F. S. Regs., Part II. and the Staff Manual respectively. Title pages will be prepared in manuscript.

Place	Date	Hour	Summary of Events and Information	Remarks and references to Appendices
Bertincourt (in the field)	1919 Feb 26		with Capt Angler ADVS inspected animals for evacuation from 235th 256th RFA 7 57th Div Amm Col. Visited Bellegise Station & arranged for trucks.	P.A.
	27		Visited VI Corps VD Qn conference with ADVS (Col Stoker). Visited 1/8 (H) Field Amb. at Ervillers. Visited Warlencourt inspected horse standings; interview with ADVS XVII Corps (Col Lake) re evacuation of animals arr Warlencourt Rly of Rossde due to a case of Epizootic Lymphangitis during being there. Capt Williams went to base P.O.	P.A.
	28		Visited Bertincourt, Achiet, Vaucourt & arranged for evacuating 30 animals to No 22 Veterinary Hospital Abbeville from Bellegise Station. Visited Dis HQ & Horse Lines.	P.A.
	29		Visited Bde HQ Qn Horse Lines & MVS. Visited 152nd Inf Bde & No 1 Sectn of 2 Remount Park (Capt Jay in care returned from leave) & MVS.	P.A.
	30		Visited Dis HQ Qn Horse Lines & MVS.	P.A.
	31		Visited Dis HQ Qn Horse Lines, visited 62 Divisional Artillery at Ytres. Visited MVS. 1/4 (H) MVS moved to Montenescourt.	P.A.

P. Nixon, Major RAVC
ADVS 57th (1st H) Division

Vol 29

War Diary.

H.A.H.Q., 51st (Highland) Division.

From 1st November, 1914 to 30th November, 1914.

Vol. XXXI

Original

Army Form C. 2118.

WAR DIARY
or
INTELLIGENCE SUMMARY.   37th (H) Division

(Erase heading not required.)

Instructions regarding War Diaries and Intelligence Summaries are contained in F.S. Regs., Part II. and the Staff Manual respectively. Title pages will be prepared in manuscript.

Place	Date	Hour	Summary of Events and Information	Remarks and references to Appendices
	1917			
Bertaucourt au Bois	Apl 1st		Visited Divisional HQ, Qr Horse Lines. Conference with P.O's	P.O.
	" 2		" " " " " Div office moved to Hermaville.	P.O.
Hermaville	" 3		" " " " Visited HQ Dr. XVII Corps. Conference with	P.O.
	" 4		C.D.V.S., A.F.A. 200 Medical. Visited Br. HQ, Qr Horse Lines	P.O.
	" 5		" " " "	P.O.
	" 6		Visited 7/(H) M.V.S at Montrencourt Visited 3 Sec. Lt. Names of Royal Seots + 4 Seaforths	P.O.
			Highlanders.	
	" 7		Visited D.D.V.S Qr Horse Lines. Visited Acheux, Louvencourt, Leabeters, Beaumont inspected 253 RFA RFH. All animals in fair condition except 'C' Bty. 255 RFA: all animals in fair condition, except 'D' Bty. Visited 52nd DAC	P.O.
	" 8		Visited Br. HQ Qr Horse Lines. Conference with P.O's	P.O.
	" 9		Visited Div. HQ Qr Horse Lines Visited Warquetin. Visited Montrencourt inspected 7(H) M.V.S. 232 M.G. Coy 1/1st Royal Scots. Animals all in good condition.	P.O.
	" 10		Went on leave to England. Capt Auger acting as A.D.V.S during my absence	P.O.
	" 11		Visited Div HQ, Qr Horse Lines + Signals. Symptoms in afternoon	27.Q.

2353 Wt. W2544/1454 700,000 5/15 D. D. & L.   A.D.S.S. Forms/C. 2118.

Original

WAR DIARY
INTELLIGENCE SUMMARY.   51st (H) Division

Army Form C. 2118.

Place	Date	Hour	Summary of Events and Information	Remarks and references to Appendices
Hermaville	1917 Nov 12		Visited Div. HQ & Horse Lines & Signals. Conference with A.D.V.S. IV Corps (Lt Harris) at Villers-au-Flos: passed 255th Bde R.F.A.; 256th Bde R.F.A.; 5.7 S.A.C. & No 1 Coy A.S.C. on return from conference on Jun animals & arranged for inspection of 16 animals from 255th Bde	P.7.Q.
"	13			P.7.Q.
			19 from 256th & 1 from Division.	
"	14		Visited Div. HQ Qr Horse lines & Signals & Passed on from at various le Corps	P.7.Q.
"	15		Visited Lns. 190 Qr Horse Lines	P.7.Q.
"	16		he returns received from Capt Donnelly: Weekly returns of horses sent to A.D.V.S. III Corps. F. (H) M.V.S. left Mondicourt for IV Corps Area staying the night of 4/17 at Couvelles-le-Comte under orders of A.S.C. 152nd Div. hit received from A.D.V.S. IV Corps at 5 pm & 6 pm A.D.V.S. to attend conference at 4th Corps HQ Qro at 11 am 17th Capt Angus on account of more sudden illness was not fit to report	P.7.Q.
"	17		A.D.V.S. Office and Staff Q. moved to Little Wood YPRES. M.V.S. was driven there on Couvelles after dark as Traffic on roads during daylight was restricted. Taken over (Q)3 of A.D.V.S. III Corps. & that F.(H) M.V.S. was here left to Beatroot Factory	P.7.Q.

Original

(3)

Army Form C. 2118.

WAR DIARY
or
INTELLIGENCE SUMMARY.

51st (H) Division

Instructions regarding War Diaries and Intelligence Summaries are contained in F. S. Regs., Part II and the Staff Manual respectively. Title pages will be prepared in manuscript.

(Erase heading not required.)

Place	Date	Hour	Summary of Events and Information	Remarks and references to Appendices
Hermaville	1917 Aug 19		RHQ visited along with 45th M.V.S., 36th Mob. Sec. & M.V.S. on first taken on to ETRICOURT. Printed orders & MVS Horse Lines	E.F.Q.
YPRES	" 19		Visited OC HQ Horse Lines. Printed RE & RA Mob Horse Lines ADVS IV Corps called. Conference with OC re carrying on evac of Sick & Wounded men. 56 Mob. Vet. area of 37th & 58th Divisions & 53rd Mob. MVS. Progress finished at	E.F.Q.
"	" 20		YPRES. 62nd Div MVS & OC re taking over of Mob. area. Printed Div. HQ. Authors Lines, RA & RE Horse Lines. Printed Div HQ RA & RE Horse Lines. ADVS IV Corps called at MVS. Conference with ADVS IV Corps. +DADVS 36th (Ulster) Division. Arrangements made for evacuation during advance. Phone calls called IV C.C.S. + OC 48th MVS re OC Capt Douglas to take the backload at YPRES. Capt Clovett A/DADVS. Guard Division called re taking over	E.F.Q. E.F.Q.
"	" 21		Visited Div HQ Horse Lines, RA & RE Horse Lines. Printed field bays at NEVILLE. For wounds sore on the sick men when in fair condition. Range was poor + only 2 Beds for any for each log.	E.F.Q.
"	" 22		Printed Div HQ Horse Lines, RA & RE Horse Lines	E.F.Q. contd

WAR DIARY
or
INTELLIGENCE SUMMARY

Army Form C. 2118.

57th (H) Division

August

Place	Date	Hour	Summary of Events and Information	Remarks and references to Appendices
YPRES	Aug 23		Returns sent to A.D.V.S. II Corps. A.D.V.S. II Corps called at Rlwhd during morning. Evacuation: D.V.S. coll. D.D.V.S. 3rd Army called Temporarily. T.E.C.: Wire recd at 12 midnight that Division was being relieved. Moving by 8.30 am on 24th. Wire replied to MVS.	2.7.0.
"	24		Orders for move did not arrive until 1.30pm. Arranged with "Q" that decken lorries at 6 Mere til 25th as most of the men were away to baths & rat annuals. Office moved to HENENCOURT. Lorries were met & towed on to BAISIEUX arriving about 8pm.	2.7.0.
HENENCOURT	25		MVS arrived in HENENCOURT half freeing move of the 57th Divl troops. Here proceeded on to BAISIEUX arriving at 9pm. arranging to Billeting for MVS.	2.7.0.
"	26		MVS moved to HENENCOURT. DADVS arrived back from leave 12 noon. Visited IV & H.Q. Hors Linses.	2.7.0. PU
BAISIEUX	27		Visited Bn.s & IV Corps Hors Lines.	PU
"	28		Visited IV Corps H.Q. at QUERRIEU. Conference with A.D.V.S. (Col Glover) visited 153 Infy Bde at ACHIEUX, Forceville, Louvencourt, Helanville, Engineers, No 3 Coy A.S.C. T/D (H) Field Amb. Mules 232 M.G.Coy. 7 Bn NR Yorks Linsen	2.7.0.

WAR DIARY
or
INTELLIGENCE SUMMARY. 57th (H) Division.

Army Form C. 2118.

Place	Date	Hour	Summary of Events and Information	Remarks and references to Appendices
BARIZEUX	1917 Nov 29th		Visited Div. H.Q., New Lines. Visited Ordnance Stores with guarantee forts. Visited M.V.S. at Mine depot. Visited R.H. & R.E. H.Q. Hope Lines. 13th used from A.D.V.S.	[illegible]
	"	30	5th Corps to send motor lorry returns on Thursday, so it was arranged. Experienced difficulty [illegible] motor hire to Ordnance Stores. Visited & inspected 151 Hy Battery at Bongancourt, stables & billets good. Visited No. 4 by A.S.C. & 232 H.D. Coy. Animals all in [illegible] condition. I arranged for No. 4 by H.S.Q. to evacuate [illegible] wounds and [illegible] horses at 132 Hy. Bn. H.Q. Horse lines.	[illegible]

P. Adam Bryn Cal.
A.D.V.S. 57 (H) Division.

WA 30

Confidential.
War Diary
of
D.A.D.V.S.
51st (Highland) Division
From 1st to 31st December, 1917.

D.A.D.V.S.
Army Form C. 2118.

WAR DIARY
or
INTELLIGENCE SUMMARY.

(Erase heading not required.)

57 (W) Division

Place	Date	Hour	Summary of Events and Information	Remarks and references to Appendices
Blargies	1919 Oct 1		Medical Board H.Q. Horse Lines, Signals; Engineers moved to Fresnicourt	P.C.
"	" 2		"	P.C.
Fresnicourt	" 3		A.D.V.S.'s Office moved to Fresnicourt. N.V.S. moved to N.H.a. Posted 132nd Infantry Bngde. Posted 3rd Portion Park.	P.C.
"	" 4		Posted 154th Infantry Bde. Posted 232nd M.G. Coy. Posted to — Portion — 3rd Portion Park. Posted Divl. M.G. Horse Lines.	P.L. P.C.
"	" 5		Quarter Evact No.Q. Horse Lines & Signals. Posted N.V.S. 2 to 3rd A. Hospl. Evact Signals of Right. Evact to animals of N.V.R. (inc— mange)	
"	" 6		Quarter Evact No Q. Horse Lines & Signals : Evact ; Evact Bngde Transport Removal of 4 Lepers to sent to — ; Posted Referencese removed of animals of 6th Batrs. Conference with A.D.S. : Evact 153rd M.G.Coy of right. 2 animals killed by bombs 7 rept wnd. Posted to H.Q. Horse Lines & Signals. Posted to Pipe line.	
"	" 7		Posted Hos P.Way Field Engrs R.E. Evacuated horses, posted — Postd to —. No R Brown, Casualties for —. Loss Coys R.E. 2rd, 4.n — Crops fair.	

Original

WAR DIARY
or
INTELLIGENCE SUMMARY.
(Erase heading not required.)

Army Form C. 2118.

51st (H) Division

Place	Date	Hour	Summary of Events and Information	Remarks and references to Appendices
Thiennes Area	1917		*Continued*	
	" 9		Visited Bde HQrs. HQ. Horse Lines; Inspected V loys HQrs at Villers au Flos. Conference with A.D.V.S. Visited 43rd (H) Field Ambulance; arrivals in good condition. Visited R.E. HQrs Horse Lines.	PC
	" 10		Inspected Div. HQ. Qr Horse Lines. Signals + R.E. HQrs. Inspected 401 Field By R.E. 7/2 (H) Field Coy. Visitols'& Inspected 1/1st Lovat Highlanders (now some HQ. Gr Horse Lines. Visited 1st & 2nd Infantry Bde, arrivals in good condition. Visited 232nd M.G. Coy. Shoeing & reports seen to B.S. Visited 1/6 Argyll & Sutherland Highlanders (just arrived). Inspected horse lines & inspected harness on arrival.	PC
	" 11		Visited 2nd HQ. Qr. Horse Lines. Visited bin shares & inspected 34 pneumonia cases. Visited MVS. Inspected R.A. Remounts (Shed as not used) Afforth. Went to Burnu to see buck left by Signals. Visited 152nd Inf. Bde.	PC
	" 12		Visited managements, manfestacturing, reports same to O.C. 1/6 (H) Field Ambulance. Inspected Bn HQ. Qr Horse Lines, Signals, R.A. HQrs & R.E. 152 Div., Inspected R.E. HQ. Horse Lines.	PC
	" 13		Visited Div. HQ. Qr Horse Lines, Inspected R.E. & P.H. HQ Horse Lines. Inspected	PC

Continued

WAR DIARY
INTELLIGENCE SUMMARY

Place	Date	Hour	Summary of Events and Information	Remarks and references to Appendices
Secunderabad	1919 Dec 13		57th I.H.C. (continued from previous)	
	14		Visited Bowl W.O. New lines; visited 134th Infy Bde. posted 400 2 451 & 400 2 Scindi Corps RB's. All necessary safeguards. Arranged for 51st IGH move to Trimulgherry. Visited hospital & 58th Cav IGH. Generals & fees condition. C.B.5 M very good.	
	15		Visited the Turghatana lines. Visited IV Corps HQrs. Conference with Col Sloan (ADVS); visited Hospitals 253 R.Bn R.W. Regiments Greatly unsatisfactory. Instructed Capt Bennett OC 1 Suspects Camp & Wing 18 Ophthalmia & 1 Surgical Case. Dr Stay will have a warrants.	
	16		Visited 4th Corps HQrs at Guy riles reported to Col Watson ADVS & inspected HQ of 49/WMK S. Visited store Signals & the 9th Gurkhas lines.	
	17		Visited store HQ Qr Horse lines. Signals - visited 4600 Mule Bn Indian cases. Horses & Ophthalmia. Visited Worley RB. General Daws & Ophthalmia cases. 1404 Coys, evacuated 4 cases of Ophthalmia. Visited 258 Ophthalmia cases, evacuated (Measured for Acuity) 3 + 2 Ophthalmia cases. Visited the HQ Qr Horse lines; Visited no 2 by 5/9th Gurkhas.	
	18		Continued	

Army Form C. 2118.

WAR DIARY
or
INTELLIGENCE SUMMARY.

(Erase heading not required.)

51st (H) Division

Instructions regarding War Diaries and Intelligence Summaries are contained in F. S. Regs., Part II. and the Staff Manual respectively. Title pages will be prepared in manuscript.

Place	Date	Hour	Summary of Events and Information	Remarks and references to Appendices
Thiennoult	1917 Jan 18 (ctd)	Continued	All arrivals in from evac'n. Visited M.V.S.; visited H.Q. Bde R.H.A.	P.a.
"	" 19		Arrivals in from evac'n. Sent P.M to evacuate + (attd) horse "A" Bty 256 Bde R.H.A. Visited brigade Q. & cage lines, signals, R.A. + R.E. H.Qrs. Visited H.Q. 40 & 152nd Infantry Bde + the Royal Scots. Visited "A" Bty Battery 255 Bde R.H.A + "C" Bty 256 Bde. Visited + inspected 5th army field artillery Res. Arrivals in from evac'n, a large number with horses skinned.	P.a.
"	" 20		Visited B.A.C. 5th Army F.A. Bde. Arrivals in very poor condition. Visited burst 140 Gr. Horse lines. Visited M.V.S. Visited 101 Debot Sqn.	P.a.
"	" 21		A.P.C. 2 animals to evacuate for mange. Conferent with A.D.S. + A.D.V.S. 5 Army Corps. "C" 255 Bde R.H.A (arrivals in from evac'n). Visited R.A. + R.E. H.Qrs No Br; visited	P.a.
"	" 22		Visited burst 140 Gr. Horse lines, signals. R.A + R.E. H.Qrs. Visited M.V.S. Visited 153rd Infy. Bde. Received + attended 153rd M.G.C. Visited 255 Bde R.H.A.	P.a.
"	" 23		Visited A.M.C.O. Horse lines. Visited 153 M.G.C. Held scrapping Received at M.V.S.	P.a.

WAR DIARY
or
INTELLIGENCE SUMMARY.

(Erase heading not required.)

Army Form C. 2118.

51st (H.) Division

Place	Date	Hour	Summary of Events and Information	Remarks and references to Appendices
	1917		*Continued*	
Hennincourt	Nov 23rd		Visited M.D.S. Visits to No 1 & No 2 Sec 1st/2nd H.F.A., 1st/3rd H.F.A. Visits to 255th Bde R.F.A.	P.M.
	24th		Lt. Andrews Clerk, injured by bomb & air raid to Etaples	
	25th		Visited Brig HQ O'Hare Lines. Visited 255 K Bde R.F.A. Visits H.Q.S. Sect. Ambulance train to inspect remounts	P.M.
	26th		Visited Bde. HQ O'Hare Lines, Signals, R.A. & R.E. Visited 255 K Bde R.F.A.	P.M.
	27th		Visited D & to M.V.S.	P.M.
	28th		Visited " " " Conference with D.O.S.	P.M.
			Inspected trolley lech	
	29th		Returned (A.F. A 2002)	P.M.
			Visited Front M.D. O'Hare Lines: Brecks to IV Corps. HQ Q1. Conference with	
			A.D.S. Pte D. O'Brien A.S.C. reported for duty as clerk to D.A.D.V.S. 51st (H.)Div.	
	30th		Visited Front HQ Pn Mons Lines. Visited 152nd Field Coy M.G. Casualties	F.M.
			amounts to 12 (5 Prisoners). 401 Hoy R.E. aviator gas: 404 Short to	
			smelling of ammunition fuses Visited 152nd M.G.Coy aviators not satisfactory	
			Great in from Cyclists. Visits 1/5 Argyll & Suth Highdrs. Edinburghs Bute 4/6	
			Gorden Highlanders Anderton pmid.	P.N.

WAR DIARY
or
INTELLIGENCE SUMMARY. 51st (H) Division

Place	Date	Hour	Summary of Events and Information	Remarks and references to Appendices
	1919		Continued	
Finmark	Jan 30		Printed award M.O. Hon Surg.; F.S.V.C.A.; Inst. 285 Bde C.A.H. Inst 1 & 2 Sections 57 b.A.C. Quoted N.V.C.	pd

P Chew Maj or 51 (H) Division
D.A.D.V.S. 51st (H) Division

Vol 31

<u>Confidential</u>

War Diary
of
D.A.D.V.S
51st Highland Division

From 1st January 1918 to 31st January 1918

Original

WAR DIARY
INTELLIGENCE SUMMARY. 51st (H) Division

Army Form C. 2118.

Place	Date	Hour	Summary of Events and Information	Remarks and references to Appendices
Steenwerck Sept	1918 1		Wrote Circul H.Q. & Horse Lines, Signals, R.E., V.L.A., M.G.Co. Wrote 255 Bde R.F.A.	P.U.
"	2		"C" Battery not attacking; several others. Wrote '8 Royal Scots T.M.B. 1/7 & 152 Bde. Wrote div HQ & Horse Lines, OA, T.M.B. M.G.Co. Wrote 8 - 255 Bde R.F.A. (16 animals Bond on "Primitive." Wrote 5th Argyll & Sutherland Highlanders, animals in good conditn.	P.U.
"	3		Wrote Div HQ Horse Lines, R.A., R.E. Signals. Wrote 1830 Infantry Bde. Conference with D.O.C.	P.U.
"	4		Wrote Div HQ D. Horse Lines, R.A. & R.E. Signals. Compiled weekly AFA 2000. Horse & Mule returns rendered separately.	P.U.
"	5		Wrote Div HQ D. Horse Lines, R.A., R.E. Signals. Wrote III Corps H.Q. Conference with A.D.V.S. Wrote to 2 Ro 51st D.T.C.	P.U.
"	6		Wrote Circul HQ D. Horse Lines, R.A., R.E. Signals. Wrote 154th Infy Bde. Wrote 15-2nd-3rd R.H. Bde (Stugzle Sutherland Hylde.) (animals in good conditn.) Wrote B. Section 51st D.T.C. all animals M.G.C. all in good conditn. Wrote B. Section 51st D.T.C. all animals in good conditn. 1 case of Opthalmia.	P.U.
"	7		Wrote Div HQ D. Horse Lines, Wrote 401st, 404th Field Coys R.E. (animals in good condn.)	P.U.

continued

WAR DIARY
or
INTELLIGENCE SUMMARY.

Army Form C. 2118.

57/21 (W) Division

Place	Date	Hour	Summary of Events and Information	Remarks and references to Appendices
1918	August 8th		Visited Div. HQ, Horse Lines, Signals, 7th DTMB; Visited 286 Bde RFA; Visited A/B, B/B 283 Bde RFA; 7th Gordons. Visited HQ 1st Bde DTC; Visited M.D.S. Visited C/Bty 255 Bde	P.Q.
"	9		Seaforth Highlanders, 7th Gordons (Animals in good condition). RFA (Animals improving). Visited Div. M.V. Horse Lines. RA R.6. Signals. Visited HQ & Horse Lines K.M. Visited "A" 285 Bde RFA. Visited 110 Bde RFA. Visited 111 Bde. 112 Bde & 2/0 Bde RFA	P.A.
"	10		Animals in good condition. Visited Div HQ. Div. Horse Lines. RA R.6. Signals. Visited Divl HQ. Conference with D.O.S.	P.Q.
"	11		Visited Div. HQ. Horse Lines; Conference with D.O.T.S. (Lt Col Clarke); Conference with D.O.C. Animals weekly A.F.B 2010	P.Q.
"	12		Visited Divl HQ. Horse Lines; R.A. R.6 & Signals. Visited III Corps HQ	P.Q.
"	13		Visited Div. HQ. Horse Lines. Visited 286-Bde RFA. Animals in good condition. Visited "C" 286 Bde RFA. Visited 1/2 W. Field Amb. Visited H.Q. 404 Field Coy RE. conclusion poor. Visited 6th Ghurkha Rifles 7 6th Leicesters. Condition good.	P.Q.
"	14		Visited M.V.S. Visited HQ D Coy 57th DTC. Inspected & Exercised (4 with Ophth.)	P.Q.

End

Army Form C. 2118.

WAR DIARY
or
INTELLIGENCE SUMMARY.
(Erase heading not required.)

572 /4/ Division

Place	Date	Hour	Summary of Events and Information	Remarks and references to Appendices
Fienvenoughs	1918	Cont	Horse Lines	
	15		Visited Div. H.Q. Horse Lines, Signals, R.H.H.C. Visited 153rd M.G.Bn, Visited B/3 R.H. Feed and. Visited G.'s 255 Bde R.H.	P.a P.a P.e
"	16		Visited Div. H.Q. Horse Lines; Visited Advd. Infantry Tunnellers re move of M.G.S. 255 Bde R.H.A. + 232 M.G.Co. Visited "C" 282 Bde R.H.A. Annual work prd. Consulted Vet. States. Visited M.S.	P.a
"	17		Visited Div. H.Q. Horse Lines. Signals. R.H.V.C. Visited 255 + 256 Bde R.H.A. Conference with DDs	P.a P.a P.a
"	18		Visited Div. H.Q. Horse Lines. Conference with A.D.V.S. H Bde Inspected Horse	P.a P.a
"	19		A.V.H. &c.	P.a
"	20		Visited 101 Lee 379 SVC TMS; Visited 256 Bde R.H.A. + Visited 153 Hy Bde	F.a
"	21		Visited Div. H.Q. Horse Lines	
			Visited Div. H.Q. Horse Lines. Pwd. Offrs to Achiet & Berles. Visited Farriers for M.S. Offrs. into Heavy A. Talking Camps at Achiet le Grand.	P.a
"	22		Visited Div. H.Q. Horse Lines; Visited M.S. with A.D.V.S. III Corps. Orde with Mayor of X. Visited attacked unit at Logeast Wood, Behagnies as intended by W.O.S. afternoon cancelled	P.a
			Cont.	

Army Form C. 2118.

WAR DIARY
or
INTELLIGENCE SUMMARY.

(Erase heading not required.)

Army of ..... 51st (H) Division .....

Instructions regarding War Diaries and Intelligence Summaries are contained in F. S. Regs., Part II. and the Staff Manual respectively. Title pages will be prepared in manuscript.

Place	Date	Hour	Summary of Events and Information	Remarks and references to Appendices
Robert Camps Rd.	1918 Jany 23		Visited Sce Off Offrs Horse Stands Lespa + 7/8 A.T. Visited No 4 Coy A.S.C. 7/M.S	P.U
	" 24		Visited 154th Infantry Bde — No 2 Coy A.S.C. at Bascaux — Boulevent Bidaumont. Conference with P.O.S. Capt Donnelly not carrying at the rations satisfactorily, cases of mange + ring worm not up to date	P.U.
	" 25		Visited S.H.Q. Horse lines. B. No 7 M.S.	P.U.
	" 26		Visited S.H.Q. Horse lines. No 5 Corp P.O.s. Conference with A.D.V.S. Corps	P.U.
	" 27		Officer returned from leave. Visited D.H.Q. Horse Lines + M.V.S. Visited 152nd Inf Bde + 400 P Battery	P.U.
	" 28		Visited Coy H.Q. Horse lines, Visited M.V.S., Visited No 4 Coy As'c. + 400 Fienth Coy	P.U.
	" 29		Visited 253rd Bde R.F.A. with A.D.V.S. Corps at Auchel Lozn	P.U.
	" 30		Visited D.H.Q. Horse lines T.M.S.	P.U.
	" 31		Visited No 3 Coy A.S.C. Conference with P.O.s	P.U.

L. Wilson Major
A.D.V.S. 51st (H) Division

D.A.D.V.S.,
51st
(HIGHLAND) DIVISION.
No. .....
3 FEB 1918

A

Vol 32

Confidential
War Diary
of
D.A.D.V.S. 51st (Highland) Division
From 1st to 28th February. 1918

Army Form C. 2118.

WAR DIARY
or
INTELLIGENCE SUMMARY. 57th (W) Division

(Erase heading not required.)

Instructions regarding War Diaries and Intelligence Summaries are contained in F. S. Regs., Part II. and the Staff Manual respectively. Title pages will be prepared in manuscript.

Place	Date	Hour	Summary of Events and Information	Remarks and references to Appendices
Aubut la Preux	1918 Sept 1		Recd 6, 250 Ford R.H. Reinforcement inspected all animals, condition good. Briefed Lieut. Hope 572 Div. Train.	P.A.
"	2		Horse Lines. Posted M.V.S. Conference with V.O.S. Inspected A.E.F. Horses. Posted Nos 3-4 Coys. 572 Div. Train	P.A.
"	3		Posted Lis. HQ Horse Lines. Held (?) V Corps V.O. D.D. Conference with DDVS. Posted M.V.S. Posted 432 M.G. Coy. Posted Nos 3-4 Coys. 572 Div. Train	P.A.
"	4		Posted 154 Fd Ambulance. Posted Bns HQ Horse lines. Posted No 2 Coy. 572 Div. Train.	P.A.
"	5		Posted 572 L.H.C. old Regimen animals in poor condition 2 evacuated in hot. Posted R.HQ Horse Lines	P.A.
"	6		Posted Bns HQ Horse Lines. Posted 253rd Bde R.F.A & I Section Siege ? Mange cases to evacuate. 18 inoculations for Pneumonia	P.M.
"	7		Posted Bns HQ Horse Lines. Posted No 3 Coy ASC inspected Departmental Horses held ? 2-4 Coys ASC. Posted 2nd Field Amb. Posted No 1 Coy. R.E. Posted 154 Inf. Bde.	P.A.
"	8		Posted Bn HQ Horse Lines RAVC V.R.O., Advd Vet Signals. Conference with V.O.C. Posted M.V.S. Nos. 2 -- 3/4 BDE. Posted Artillery H.B.	P.A.
"	9		Posted V, HQ Horse Lines. Conference AEF 2 evac. Posted II Corps V.H. V.O. Conference with DDVS. Posted M.V.S. with Major Horners 572 Div.	P.A.

(Continued.)

WAR DIARY
or
INTELLIGENCE SUMMARY.

Army Form C. 2118.

(2)

57 (H) Division

(Erase heading not required.)

Place	Date	Hour	Summary of Events and Information	Remarks and references to Appendices
Steenwerck	Sept 1915 9		Continued. 25 Hrs en taking over. Duties for W.D. those lines.	P.C.
"	10		Duties for W.D those lines. Details to 3 Coy. R.E. inspite assessment. Duties R.E. Battn. important transport from the left flank. Made attempt to inspect transport from the west.	P.U.
"	11		Details to Div Horse Lines. Duties to 2 Coy. O.E.E. Duties to R.A. Horse Lines Batmen.	P.U.
"	12		Examined Reference Div Lines. Duties to W.D. those lines. Capt Taylor back went in lorry 94/R 6 2946. Details to 218.	P.U. P.U.
Steenwerck	13		Cops ASE. Duties to W.D those lines.	
"	14		Duties to the Defence Lines. Details 152 Inf. Bde. "400" + "401" Field Coys R.E. Duties 255 R.S. H.H. (RBT & others) and 57 W. Field Amb.	P.U.
"	15		Duties to W.D. those lines R.A. R.E. Supplies. Duties to Veterinary inspects animals. Cropped B.C. H. man.	P.U. P.U.
"	16		Duties to W.D. those lines. Duties to Corps HQP Conference with DDS (Colonel) Duties 151 Inf. Bde. at Bunga, Steenwerck. Duties to 11/2 Relain BC. + 57 Bn 255 Bn H H.	P.U.
"	17		Duties /B (N) Field Amb 57 Royal Scots. Continued	P.C.

Army Form C. 2118.

WAR DIARY
or
INTELLIGENCE SUMMARY.

(Erase heading not required.)

Place	Date	Hour	Summary of Events and Information	Remarks and references to Appendices
Suivincourt	1915			
	Feb 18		[illegible handwritten entries]	P.A.
	19			P.A.
	20			P.A.
	21			
	22			P.A.
	23			P.A.
	24			P.A.
	25			P.A.

WAR DIARY
or
INTELLIGENCE SUMMARY.

Army Form C. 2118.

Place	Date	Hour	Summary of Events and Information	Remarks and references to Appendices
Arras	1918			

Vol 33

Confidential
War Diary
of 51st Division
D.A.D.V.S. 51st Division
from 1st to 31st March 1918.

WAR DIARY
INTELLIGENCE SUMMARY.

Army Form C. 2118.

Place	Date	Hour	Summary of Events and Information	Remarks and references to Appendices
France	1/8		Brought Div HQ G. Home lines R.A. R.E. M.G. Qr. HQ signals. Divn to 255th & 256th Bdes R.F.A.	P.Q.
"	2		Bn to M.T.S. Divn to Royal Sects Canadian Inmounted pnrs. Bn to S.H.Q. Home lines R.A.M.C. M.G. signals. Divn to 255 & 256 Bdes. Bn to 300 407 409 Field Coys medicals in pub ambulance. Bn to m Bn divn + 19 Argylls (arrivals in fort today). Bn to 24 CW Field Ambulance. Bn to S.H.Q. Home lines R.A., R.E., T. signals.	P.Q.
"	3		Bn to 255² + 256 Bdes R.F.A. 1 Com attached A.Y. 1 Com C. 258 Bde. Bn to M.G. M.T.S. 3 Pomeths arrived Bn to S.H.Q. Home lines R.A. + R.E. H.Qrs. signals. Bn to A.T.S. Fund Hos 1 + 2 lectures S.H.C. to 1 lecth. mon-clean of charge Bn to 255 + 256 Bn. R.F.A. Bn to 57 + M.C. Bus arrivals in fort considers 2 A.M.	P.Q.
"	4			P.Q.
"	5		Bn to S.H.Q. Home lines R.A. R.E. H.Q.+ T. signals. Bn to 255² + 256 Bde R.F.A. Bn to 3 sec O.T.C. Divn to 152² duty Bde + 43 (W) Field Amb. (quite a very soft total).	P.Q.
"	6		Bn to S.H.Q. Home lines R.A. R.E. Signal Divn to 154 R.F.A. Bde Bn to 152nd Duty Bde (arrivals in post considers in ecklow Divn to 256 Bde	P.Q.

Continued

Army Form C. 2118.

WAR DIARY
or
INTELLIGENCE SUMMARY.
(Erase heading not required)

57th (H) Division

Instructions regarding War Diaries and Intelligence Summaries are contained in F. S. Regs., Part II. and the Staff Manual respectively. Title pages will be prepared in manuscript.

Place	Date	Hour	Summary of Events and Information	Remarks and references to Appendices
Steenwerck	1918 Sept 4		Bde to 1/4 D.H. Conv R.H.A. & Signals, Bde to 255 & 256 Bde R.T.A. Welcome message to D.S.O.R. Bde to 1/5 (W) Field Amb. Letter	P.a.
	5		Circular from B Battery Bde to 1st Bn 2 C/Os & W.O.s, Bde to 255 & 256 Bde R.T.A.	P.a.
			Conference wh. P.O.s	P.a.
	9		Bde to D.H.Q. Wire from R.H.R.E. Signals, Wire to III Corps Adft. Conference	P.a.
	10		Bde H.O.S., Bde to 153 Inf Bde, Bde (W) Home lines & Signals, Bde to M.L.S. General Transport Conference Turning Catapults. Bde to 255 & 256 Bde R.T.A. Wire to No1 Sec F.Q.	P.a.
	11		Visits D.M.Q. Home lines. Visit 154 Inf Bde Bde to 400, 401 & 402 Field Cos. Visits D.Q. (W) Field Amb. Bde to M.L.S. 21 Lieutenants for Co.	P.a. P.a.
	12		Visit Inf. & Arty Bde to 6 H.Q. Elaborate, Bde to 255 & 256 Bde R.T.A. Wire to 1st Dep. Bde to B.H. Intelligence Bde to 1/3 (W) Field Amb. Bde to 255 & 256 Bde R.T.A.	P.a.
	13		Conference with P.O.s re case change. R 255 + one in D 255 Bde 156 R.H.L. Bde Capt. Unger D.L.C. went on special leave to Rd. Stand. Corps	P.a.

Original

Army Form C. 2118.

WAR DIARY
or
INTELLIGENCE SUMMARY.

(Erase heading not required.)

57th (W) Division (3)

Instructions regarding War Diaries and Intelligence Summaries are contained in F. S. Regs., Part II. and the Staff Manual respectively. Title pages will be prepared in manuscript.

Place	Date	Hour	Summary of Events and Information	Remarks and references to Appendices
Fromont	Feb 14 1918		Visits Lieut D.O. Horse Lines R.A. R.E. Signals, Trains 255 + 256 Bde R.F.A. Visits M.D.S. Visits Post at Bettes et R.A.	Nil
	15		Visits on H.Q. Horse Lines, Visits 2/1 (W) Field Amb. Visits 153 + 154 Bde, Visits 401 Field Coy + sat Labourers Employed MFP 2000	Nil
	16		Visits Div HQ Horse Lines. Visits Corps HQ conference with D.D.M.S. Visits Pay Imprest 4000 4001 Field Cys. Visits 1/2 (W) Field Amb. Visits 256 Bde	Nil
	17		Visits the Montine Caves Visits M.F.C. + No 3 & M.S.	Nil
			R.F.A.	
	18		Visits Stores for Unwadin R.A. R.E. Signals, Visits 1/3 (W) Field Amb Visits 256th Bde R.F.A. 3 new Umaste and Visits 154th Ay Bde	Nil
	19		Visits on H.Q. Horse Lines R.A. R.E. Signals, Visits M.D.S. Visits	Nil
	20		255 Bde R.F.A. re close range B 255 Bde. Visits 64 n.S. Coy Visits on Div O Horse Lines R.A. R.E. Signals. Visits M.D.S. 33 arrivals Returns to duty after fumigation. Visits 255th + 257 Bde RFA.	Nil
	21		Visits of H.Q. Horse Lines Signals German attack commenced. 3 arrivals Visits on Signals Visits M.D.S. moves to Ablu at Post	Nil
			Cont	

Army Form C. 2118.

WAR DIARY
or
INTELLIGENCE SUMMARY.

(Erase heading not required.)

51st (H) Division

Place	Date	Hour	Summary of Events and Information	Remarks and references to Appendices
Achiet le Petit	1918 Mar 22		Major xxx the Div. Brig. heavily shelled at night	p.a.
	23		Divnl M.S. at Brig relievs arranged for evacuation for 58 wounded	p.a.
	24		from Armoured Station	
			1 Q — to M.S.C.	
	25		went to Pasturement with Div Brig	p.g.
	27		" " A.D.D.S. interviews with A.D.S.	p.a.
			Marieux	p.t
	28		Went to Bordeau joined M.S. went to Renaucourt & Amiens M.S at	p.c.
			Baizy, arrangd for move to Amiens and 154 Inty Bde	p.a.
	29		Move to Tongueres & opened Office. Report to A.D.D.S. 1st Corps	p.a.
	30		M.S. at Layet	p.a.
	31		M.S. moves to Thieuguval report arrival france to A.D.D.S. III Corps	p.a.
			Arrived 1352 Inty Bde.	p.a.

P.Chan Major A.D.M.S 51st Division

D.A.D.M.S.
51st
(HIGHLAND DIVISION)
No. 4/8
Date 4 APR 1918

War Diary
of
DADVS 51st (H) Division
for
April 1918

Army Form C. 2118.

WAR DIARY
or
INTELLIGENCE SUMMARY. 51/2 (W) Division

(Erase heading not required.)

Instructions regarding War Diaries and Intelligence Summaries are contained in F. S. Regs., Part II. and the Staff Manual respectively. Title pages will be prepared in manuscript.

Place	Date	Hour	Summary of Events and Information	Remarks and references to Appendices
Auguez	1918 April 1		Brestation 300 O.R. Lieutenance R.A. R.F. Signals + M.F.S. 1 Offrs + 40 O.R. interviews with Col. re transport ADMS. Visits no 4 toy 51st Div Train. Visits Brig to Brigade + half Brigades	P.a.
	2		Visits ADM. Field Tent. arranged for evacuation. Capt. Ingles A.B.S. 85/HM.F.S. returned from leave (General). Visits + B.S.M. of those Lines R.E. + R.A. Signals. O.C.T.S. follow-ups called	P.a.
	3		Visits Div. Ord. Arms Div. P. Ay's. Store Bombed 2 Artillery Horses killed + 1 orderlies wounded by R.E. O. The wound deliberately attended from no later. Visits 401 Field Coy at Labeuvay. Visits No. 1 + 2 Section 51st DAC at Lindeux	P.B.
	4		Visits RES H.O. House Lines R.F. R.F. Signals. Visited M.S. arranged for take over 31st Div 2ns or Bray. Visits ODRS. D.E.G.R. Inspection with B.C.s	P.a.
	5		Visits Div to Ordnance Lines. R.A./ R.E Signals + Field Ambulance. Com. Complete R.F.A. Cows. Officer moves to Lebeuvay. M.J.S. moves to Burbure. 6 been reposted from 16 no Poly. Hospital Round (no arms) for deity will M.S. were detained on the F.R. but not injured	P.a.
	6		Visits 255th Bar B.F.A. at Mazette. Letters home re her evacuation + he was carried with Capt Emmett RAMC very involuntarily having no such laws in "B" By DC case	P.a.

A 5534. W W/4973/M657. 750,000. 8/16. D.D.&L.Ltd. Forms/C.2118/13

Army Form C. 2118.

WAR DIARY
or
INTELLIGENCE SUMMARY.   57½ M/ Burner
(Erase heading not required.)

Instructions regarding War Diaries and Intelligence
Summaries are contained in F. S. Regs., Part II.
and the Staff Manual respectively. Title pages
will be prepared in manuscript.

Place	Date	Hour	Summary of Events and Information	Remarks and references to Appendices
INFANTRYIERE			Quiet day. Attempted MORE T Borgne offensive does not operate; Limits not used get. "A" Bty 5 rounds in one direction. Practice 238 Field T.H. (Imp not satisfactory 26 pos "B" pos	
	7		A not anything. 26 C Sept – "D" not satisfactory. Recent Tracks in Large Kilo entrenchment with R/ES. Renewal AFA 2000	P.C.
			Practice bis M.O. Chas Lieu. Practice 57 Marching Son Bn. at ATHIESIN. Practice 46 Surgical field ambs. Balls fight.	P.C.
	8		Practice bis NO British from NE Hynes. Officer moved MOBECO (Bellow?) within Limits to AFICS XI Corps. (Retirement covered). Drinking bis MO Br.Amb.Aux T.Hynes. T H.O. Field Cor. R.S. "S"	P.C. P.C.
	9		Officer moved to HAM EN ARDIS. Practice MIS at MONO DE VILLE	P.C. P.C.
HAM	10		Practice M.I.S. Conference with D.D.s (Corps Angles Arty General)	
	11		Practice M.I.S. came moved to FONTES. Practice 118 AFA 2000 (offensive in progress retirement in such active operation). Practice 526 at BRUNES. Practice 182nd Brig Field	
	12		401 Field Covey (covered retr? ? permission). Practice uses field Coy. 1/3 + 2/5 (H) Field Amts. (arranged in for aircraft)	
	13		Practice x/ Corps. H.Q.S conference with R.D.S. Col. Coltrane. Practice M.I.S. orchest. C.W.T.	P.C.

Army Form C. 2118.

Original

WAR DIARY
or
INTELLIGENCE SUMMARY. 31st (W) Division.
(Erase heading not required.)

Instructions regarding War Diaries and Intelligence
Summaries are contained in F. S. Regs. Part II
and the Staff Manual respectively. Title pages
will be prepared in manuscript.

Place	Date	Hour	Summary of Events and Information	Remarks and references to Appendices
Heav—	April 13	(cont)	Wrote to 110 Brittain Grove	P.2.
"	14		Wrote 401 Field Coy. Wrote 1/3 (W) Field Amb. 152 + 153rd Inty. Bdes (arrangements re graves Correction) Wrote 3028 2 + 3 Echelon GHQ.	P.2.
"	15		Wrote 401 Field Coy. GHQ. arranged to obtain an echo field. D.H.O wrote	P.A.
"			LANDRÉCIES	
"	16		Wrote L 340 other BRIGADES. Wrote to 2 Echelon GHQ. 154 R.Bty Bde (front candidate) Wrote 401 + 2nd Field Coys. Wrote to 39 Divnl M.G. Coy. (wrote — graves Condition.)	P.U.
"	17		Wrote to 39th M.G. Bn. (arrival with proposals of front) Wrote 401 Field Coy. (received information) Wrote 110 Field Bty. Wrote 1/3 (W) Field Amb. + 9/0 (W) field (amb.) Wrote 152 R.Bty Bde. Wrote to 2 Echelon GHQ (only per echelon) Wrote to sing point Wrote to 2 Echo. GHQ. Wrote 4001 + 402nd Field Coy.	P.12.
"	18		Wrote 253rd Bde R.F.A. (another presently prior recieved him " B" Bty. Clear change. not recorded. Damaged unusable brouisel for wounds See appdx here seen to jet M.V.S. to W.Ust. & 2 Rnsys. Wrote 258 Bde R.F.A. (correction previously prior, Several turn Amb+ Amb+ amb, transported week of 4.) (4) Conference ack". P.08.	P.12.

A S 8 34 Wt W4953/M687 750,000 8/16 D. D. & L. Ltd. Forms/C.2118/13.

Original

WAR DIARY
or
INTELLIGENCE SUMMARY. 51st Wr Division
(Erase heading not required.)

Army Form C. 2118.

Instructions regarding War Diaries and Intelligence Summaries are contained in F. S. Regs., Part II. and the Staff Manual respectively. Title pages will be prepared in manuscript.

Place	Date	Hour	Summary of Events and Information	Remarks and references to Appendices
Maur	1916 July 20		Orders to 61st Div. Visited M.V.S. Visited 1/2 Hy Field Amb. (London gnd)	P.U.
"	21st		Visited 1/2 Hy Field Amb. No.1 Sec. 2770. 134 F Supp. Sec. 401st Field Ambce R.E. Hospital	P.U.
"	21st		Visited 401st F.A 19 taken by N.F. Visited 312th Machine Gun By Animals in pond conditions	P.U.
"	22nd		Visited 256th Bn RFA (considered favourably pm). 2 cases of Mumps in B By left outside. Visited 258 Bn RFA Animals generally in fair condition.	P.U.
Norrent Fontes	23rd		Main Office moved to NORRENT FONTES (Billet 3b). Visited R.O 4 By & 154 Farm Amp Sec. 134 Manure and urine satisfactory. Visited x1 Corps No3 & 4 Veterinary Column and ADVS. Visited M.V.S.	P.U.
"	24th		Visited 540 Home Unit RE & Signals. Visited M.V.S. & 154th Supp Sec. Court-Martial & 1/6 6 Hy Corps Siege Bde Horses.	P.U.
"	25th		Visited 540 Horse Unit & M.V.S. Visited Corps Euracuating Station to meet DAV.S. 1st Army (Col. Saunders) Troops & Corps. Winter afternoon. M.V.S. and Horses & Colts. Stalls and Urgent Occur.	P.U. 21
"	26th		Visited the Belgian Units & Signals. Enquiries AFB2000. A.D.V. ercles.	Enforced

A 5834 Wt. W 4973/M687. 750,000. 8/16 D. D. & L. Ltd. Forms/C.2118/13.

Army Form C. 2118.

WAR DIARY
or
INTELLIGENCE SUMMARY.

572/(H) Division

(Erase heading not required)

Place	Date	Hour	Summary of Events and Information	Remarks and references to Appendices
Grand Ravine	1918 April 29		Inst. A.D.V.S. 410 Horse shoes stopped (one consignment) — Rain to-day spoilt A.D.V.S, M.V.S. No 3 & 4 Coys. 510 Bn Tren. 408 Tren. Coy. No 1 & 2 Orders 372-H2 to 5th Machine Gun Bn.	P.O.
	28		Posted Orr. Vet. Or House Lines to M.V.S.	P.O.
	29		Visited No 155 Co Horse lines. Posted 1 inspector to 336 Businessmen Pl. Under 218 Br. Coy. (names & numbers furnished in foregoing inspection) Cadet 278 Br. Coy. P.O.	P.O. P.O.
	30		Rec'd Div. V.O. Or Horse Lines "C" "G" "E" Coys. 6 1/2 M.V.S. + M.V.S. + 152 Bty. Bde.	P.O.

D.A.D.V.S.
51st
(HIGHLAND DIVISION)
No. Y/575
Date 30 APR 1918

M.V.S. Mustered Aug 4th 1914
get recd'd service 30th April 1918
was approved D.A.D.V.S. 51st Division June 30th 1917

P. Alison Prifer
D.A.D.V.S. 51st (H) Division

Confidential. No. 35

War Diary
of
D.A.D.V.S. 51st (H) Division
from 1st to 31st May. 1918.

WAR DIARY / INTELLIGENCE SUMMARY

Army Form C. 2118.

57 (W) Division

Place	Date	Hour	Summary of Events and Information	Remarks and references to Appendices
Forest l'Abbaye	May 1st		Visited forward Hd Qr Horse Lines R.E. & Signals. Visited Mob Veterinary Section	P.A.
"	2nd		Routes " "	P.A.
			Visited XVII Corps 57 Div Troop Train. Conference with D.O.S.	
"	3rd		Visited Hd Qr Horse Lines; MVS. No 1, 2 & 3 Sections 57 D.A.C.; 1/3 (W) Field Ambulance; Conferred R.E. & Signals	P.A.
"	4th		Visited M.V.S.; 153 Infy Bde; 1/3 (W) Field Amb.; Div Hd Qr Horse Lines & Certain None	P.A.
"	5th		Visited Div Hd Qr Horse Lines; MVS. No 3 Section DHQ at Mhow & No 4 Coy 57 Div Train	P.A. P.A.
	6th		Div Office moved from Forest l'Abbaye to Morcuil	P.A.
			Visited 57 D.V. Horse Lines R.E. & Signals. Visited ADMS XVII Corps at Guieuse; interviewed with Lt Col Loke OVC. Visited MVS.	P.A.
Morcuil	7th		Visited Div Hd Qr Horse Lines. Visited Stores & arranged path from Hqrs for Camp for MVS. Visited MVS. Visited ADVS Corps	P.A.
"	8th		Visited MVS. Visited R.E. & Signals.	P.A.
"	9th		Visited Div Hd Qr Horse Lines R.E. & Signals. Visited MVS with ADVS Corps. Conference with DOS.	P.A.
			Continued	

Army Form C. 2118.

Original

WAR DIARY
or
INTELLIGENCE SUMMARY.

51st Division

(Erase heading not required.)

Instructions regarding War Diaries and Intelligence Summaries are contained in F.S. Regs., Part II. and the Staff Manual respectively. Title pages will be prepared in manuscript.

Place	Date	Hour	Summary of Events and Information	Remarks and references to Appendices
Maxwell	1918 May 10		Continued. Visited Bde HQ & Horse Lines R.E. & Signals. Visited 201st Field Coy R.E. animals not in very good condition. Visited 31st Bde from HQ Div inspects them. Ditto	P.A.
"	" 11		M.T.S. Camp ditto A.F.A 2000. Visited M.T.S. Visited No 2 by road, saw inspects "Kemmel". Visited 152nd Infy Bde " 153rd Infy Bde. Visited Div HQ & Horse Lines R.Es & Signals.	P.A.
"	" 12		Visited Div HQ & Ordnance R.E. & Signals. Visited two Field Coy R.E. animals in good condition. Instructs Capt A. Donnelly M.G. Inspect to this effice or this 13 day for interview with G.O.C. Div. (Brigr General S.J.C. Carter - Campbell D.S.O)	P.A.
"	" 13		Visited Bde HQ Or Horse lines R.Es & Signals. Visited h.v.s. 152nd & 154th Infy Bdes. & / . (H) Field Amb. & 153rd Batty Bde with ADVS Corpl Red Lake. Capt Donnelly arr reports & was interviewed by G.O.C. re accurate report.	P.A.
"	" 14		Visited Div HQ Or Horse Lines. 1/8 (H) Field Amb. Visited 401 Field Coy. 37 Bn 8 Bn & Infantry Details at Scene. (Animals in good condition). 400 Field Coy animals in fair condition.	P.A.
"	" 15		Visited Div. HQ Or Horse Lines R.Es & Regts. Visited 152nd Infy Bde(Anl .I) & M.V.S. Visited & inspected No 1 Coy 15th Bn Train (animals in good condition)	P.A.

Continued

WAR DIARY
INTELLIGENCE SUMMARY.

Army Form C. 2118.

51st (H) Division

Place	Date	Hour	Summary of Events and Information	Remarks and references to Appendices
Signal	1918		Continued	
Boiseleux	May 16		Visited Bdes H.Q. & Hone lines R.E. & Signals. Visited 7/8 Royal Scots. Ascertained in fair condition; visited & inspected 7/8 Black Watch, 15 Veterans. Ascertained in fair condition. Conference with P.O.'s. Visited M.F.S. Conference P.O.s.	P.W.
"	"17		Visited 5th/7th Gordon lines R.E.S. & Sigs. Visited M.F.S. Horse lines & transport. Completed A.F.A. B.2010.	P.W.
"	"18		Visited Bdes H.Q. 5th/7th Hone lines R.E. & Signals. Visited transport 15-R. RHA.	P.W.
"	"19		at Bdy. Accounts in fair condition. Visited Corps Holds Conference with Assrs. Visited 6th/7th Dr Horse lines R.E. & Sigs. Visited M.F.S. 3 men were dispatched from R.V.S. to XVIII Corps Remounting Station at Jerusalem prior to Base on reduction of Establishment. Visited 7/8 Royal Scots.	P.W.
"	"20		Visited 7th/7th Dr Horse Lines R.E.'s Signals. Visited Canine Transports.	P.W.
"	"21		401 Field Coy (Accounts in improving) 400 Field Coy Accounts fair condition. Visited 404 Field Coy at Boiseleux fair condition; Visited H.Qrs 51st M.C.Coy. Visited 152, 153, 154 Infty Bdes at Hq & Services. Visited M.F.S.	P.W.
"	"22		Visited 6th/7th Dr Horse lines R.E. & Sigs. Visited No 1 Mounted Shuffle School 4/7 Royal Scots, Cartridges Horse + M.F.S. 51st D.B. at Boiry. Continued	P.W.

WAR DIARY
INTELLIGENCE SUMMARY. 51—W Burrow

Army Form C. 2118.

Place	Date	Hour	Summary of Events and Information	Remarks and references to Appendices
Morcenil	1918 May 22	Continued	Capt G/Major ADS Meulen in exspectation	P.H.
	23		Visited Bn HQ Qr Horse Lines R8 Flys 1st Bn HS, 16 Royal Scots, 404th Field Coy RE & Tuilleau horse. Males arr inspected 152 Inf. Bde Conference. Coll D.D.R.	P.H.
	24		Visited Bn HQ W. Qr Horse Lines R8's Flys Divisional Corps M.O's Conference will ADR re Veterinary Evacuating Station etc Brutes MS Arrive 104 Cy, 370 Bn Train. Inspected remounts Inspected WT F2000. Visited Hqs M.O.Qr stores lines R8's Flys SF 2352-50 16 Royal Scots. Bruts MS. Above billet, stores etc burnt at MHS. All was supported.	P.H.
	25		Visited Bn HQ MO Qr stores lines R8's Flys Tuilleau Farm. 513/104 Field Amb. Summer inspection for field units. Visited MS. Arrange for	P.H.
	26		Enquiry re fire Visited Bn HQ Qr Horse Lines. R8's Flys Arrange for ADS & Inspected BnHQ. E Qury Held at MHS as to cause of fire	P.H.
	27		Funerals of Drivers Major Stan 370 Bn Train, President (with MS & Tuilleau Farm Visited 570 Inf S. Bn. (D.Coy Not very good) Continued	P.H.

Army Form C. 2118.

WAR DIARY
or
INTELLIGENCE SUMMARY.
(Erase heading not required.)

Army: 51st (H) Division

Place	Date	Hour	Summary of Events and Information	Remarks and references to Appendices
Moreuil	1918 Mar 28		Visited Div. H.Q. Horse Lines, R&S Regs, Veterinary stores, Mobile Vet. Sec. Visits MRS & 153rd Bdy Bde.	PH
"	29		"	PH
"			Moreuil Line	
"	30		Visited Div H.Q. A. Horse Lines R&S & Regs. Conference will DDS reserves with ADVS.	PH
"	31		Visited Div HQ A. Horse Lines R&S Regs. Visited MRS. Visited Div Staff. Copied AFF2600. Arranged for Horse Transport to be erected at MRS. Received instructions for A/S/Sgt Munro R AVC 1/4/H/A M.S. to be Transferred to XVII Corps Forwarding Station on reduction of Establishment	PH

P Aken Major AVC
DADVS 51st (H) Division

Confidential

War Diary
of
A.D.V.S. 51st (H) Division
for June 1918.

WAR DIARY
INTELLIGENCE SUMMARY.

Army Form C. 2118.

51st W. Division

Place	Date	Hour	Summary of Events and Information	Remarks and references to Appendices
Mitteal	June 1st 1915		Visited Allonagne & inspected 51st Div: Head Qrs on first arrival. No 1 Section... to 2 Sect... then Visited Brewers area inspected 255th & 236th Bdes RFA. 255th A Bty condition fair. "B" Bty good "C" Ammunition ford. Noticed "D" Ammunition good. 236 Bde A Bty condition good. No fair. "B" condition good. I then visited "C" Bty condition good. Same "D" Bty condition good.	P.A.
"	2nd		Visited 70 Field RFA 15 Brunner all in good condition. Visited Div H Qrs None Lines Regt Signals	P.A.
"	3rd		Visited BAC. wagon Lines RH Bty nole. Visited Wagons 51st RH & Br amunion good. Visited & inspected 15 Royal Scots Amunion good. Visited Gordons Horse Shipping & Parker to MC reported for duty with 2 150 shells RFA Wagons from 6 RHa reported for duty with 154 Duty Bde	P.A.
"	4th		Visited all lines of terriers two battery unit CAMS XII Corps (Col Lake arc) & inspected of all amunition, condition very good. General inspecting	P.A.
"	5th		Just feet with Coln.	P.A.
"	6th		Visited Div H.Q. Horse Lines R.E.T. Signals. Visited M.S. Visited Div 51st H.Q. Horse Lines R.E. H.Q. Signals. Conference with Q.O.S. (Continued)	P.A.

Army Form C. 2118.

WAR DIARY
or
INTELLIGENCE SUMMARY. 372 (W) Division
(Erase heading not required.)

Place	Date	Hour	Summary of Events and Information	Remarks and references to Appendices
Havincourt	1916 Aug 7		Continued. Maj Gen W.H. Rivers RBS Kingscote Kenshaw Gen. Congreve DFA D.O.O.	PH
"	8		Went to line to reylard since 8.6.2.9.0 westerly 50 bts 7 AFS XVII Corps. Then aid autotrailed to Capt Asper MC Oct. R.A.M.C. Took over 10 miles of front army from Eric Lubeur in Line August from 6 Refraining units Representing from Rest Camp - 400 + 100 4 the Field Tops RE 4/6 Royal Scots	PH
"	9		Posted S.A.A. dump 57-25.6d.9.0. 1 killed wounded. Aireed Home Rest Camp suspect all reinorcts (35 Lmen 4 mutes) for wheeling Names. Maties M+5 territine 8.7.0 Farm. Lt Col Nr Home Luis + 5 Lt N.D.O.W. (en along home pass)	8.7.0
"	10		Posted Div HQ HQ ten Lines Kingscote (Van Loon). Posted all transport Lives and Inf and M+S Ambulns lines t/3 (W) Field Ambulnce Dinner at Contalmaison Farm 1 WM Nam	8.7.0
"	11		Posted Div HQ HQ ten Line Kegs 73(W) Field amb, 404-Field By RE, Canteen Stores also 152 Lty Bde (Horse all trying well. Posted 285 Bde HQ. Div 2 Le DAC all men in pretty inspired in crickts	8.7.0
"	12		Continued	8.7.0

Army Form C. 2118.

WAR DIARY
or
INTELLIGENCE SUMMARY.
(Erase heading not required.)

57 (W) Divison

Place	Date	Hour	Summary of Events and Information	Remarks and references to Appendices
Morval	1918 June 12	Ordinary	3 cases of mange in "C" Bty; 1 in "A" Bty; visited Div. HQ Horse Lines Signals.	57.9.A.
"	13		15-Browns (lame horse) + M.T.S.; Inspected Knapsack lines in Back area will view to preventative measures taken against Mobile Bombing. Made arrangement to send suspected Glow cases to Fienvylet.	
"	14		Visited 440 Art & Signals Horse Lines; M.V.S.; 1st Royal Scots + 51 M.G. Bn; visited Div H Qr Horse Lines Signals; 70 Royal Scots + M.V.S. Visited 153 Inf. Bde Transport Lines (most of animals not grazing) Inspected the Remounts at no 3 Bty to Draw before despatch. Sent sick H.F.A. 200 letters.	57.9.A. 57.9.A.
"	15		Visited M.V.S.; 256 Bde R.F.A; 1 case Deep Mange A Bty; ordered to be sent to 1 in "B"; 4 in "C" also sent to M.V.S. for evacuation. 12 animals inoculated. Visited 255 Bde R.F.A. 1 case Mange C Bty. Sent to Fienvylet; Visited XVII Corps HQ Gras Patrol of Engineers. Visited H.Q.R.A. Signals; M.V.S. + 153 Inf. Bty Bde.; Inspected all horses at 255 Bde R.F.A. which were sent to M.V.S. for treatment in Fienvylet. 4 of which Evacuated. (2 from B/255 - 2 from C/255; 40 of cases sent (Fienvylet) 3 from C/255 - 3 from D/255; 4 from B/256) visited Airdrome Horse (sick)	57.9.A. 57.9.A.

Continued

WAR DIARY or INTELLIGENCE SUMMARY

Army Form C. 2118.

57/91/W Burnier

Place	Date	Hour	Summary of Events and Information	Remarks and references to Appendices
Marieul	1918 June 17		Visited HQTS XVII Corps at 9:30am. Visited 57 Divn M.G. Bn.; 1/8 Royal Scots; 152 Bdy. Bde. M.V.S. No case Evy. change evacuated from A/DMS	E.F.A.
"	18		Visited Divn HQ. 102 A.Amn Sub Park; 404 Field Coy R.E. (New installations) Visited 401 Field Coy; A Coy 57 M.G. Bn (no case gastritis?). Visited M.V.S. 1/A/255 Bde R.F.A.	E.F.A.
"	19		Visited 2 O. 12 Billet Marieul + arranged for extension of horse lines by A/152 Bde R.F.A.; Visited 1/3 (H) Field Cast.; S.A.A. Lu. 57 Divn.; M.V.S. + 153 Bdy. Fd. Amb.	E.F.A.
"	20		Visited M.V.S. + 152 Sdy. Bde. 110 Qrs + signals. Returns from D.O.S. + Conference. Visited 404 Coy R.E. Inspected Dettby horse at XVII Corps Restcamp. Sent Maun to M.V.S. 5th Funtd in Furigate.	E.F.A.
"	21		Visited 1/3 (H) Field Cast. (1 Lymphagitis Case) Visited Signals (1 Anne horse) Visited M.V.S.; 16 Hmm. sent to Furuyati from 255 Bde. 3 kept at M.V.S. further treatment. Returns sent to HQ'S XVII Corps.	E.F.A.
"	22		Visited 255 Bde R.F.A. (14 animals veined live and to M.V.S. 2:30 pm husband in Furuyati. Visited M.V.S.; XVII Corps Rest Camp + inspected 20 Coy Inch. (all animals in excellent condition)	E.F.A.

(Continued)

WAR DIARY / INTELLIGENCE SUMMARY

Army Form C. 2118.

51st (H) Division

Place	Date	Hour	Summary of Events and Information	Remarks and references to Appendices
Marcel	June 23 1917		N.to 286 H.Bde R.F.A. (3 hours) Sent to Trumpeter. Return in 13" 1 from C. & 1 from B. 5 Batteries. D.to 153 App. Bde.; 51 M.G.Bn 4 Mks. Inspected 20 horses sent from 255 Batt RHA for trumpet — 2 from A which remain for further trial. 5 from B. 10 from C. 3 from B. Noted to be the others. 2 cases of urged mange to trips for examination. In all breaches. Noted arrangements for evacuation. Noted arrangements for horses being evacuated. Gave to the Supplies list. Owners to all the Bde regarding Mange.	270
"	24		Arrived back from leave. Took over duties of DDVS from Capt Angler CAVC. Inspected No 2 Lc. Effs.; D.to XVII Corps 10 Bn experience with CCVS. Visited the 75th Gl. How Batts. Arranged for inspection of Artillery by AVS through P.to — Do 10 Mtn How Bde. R.F. 106 Brigade. 255 Bde R.F.A. missing in a.m.	PH
"	25		For purpose of new inspection. Conference with DDS.	PH
"	26		Visited OC of the W/O conference with TMS or mostly Administrative. Brig: WLS arranged well. Saw some orders to be circulated. Deems one for destroyed. Visited W/O GH Mess. Saw one letter from 255 Bde R.F.A. Mange reduces to be evacuated. Visited WH W/O D on inspection of mange before etc. Continued	P.H.

Continued

Army Form C. 2118.

WAR DIARY
or
INTELLIGENCE SUMMARY. 57-(?) Division

(Erase heading not required.)

Place	Date	Hour	Summary of Events and Information	Remarks and references to Appendices
Miraval	1918 June 27		Visited & examined watering all animals in 255 Bee RFA. Ordered the evacuation of suspects mange 1 from A, 1 from B, 1 from C, 1 from D hi. All new arrivals in Fort Camelon, No instruction in AVC Reg. 4 rules "B" Battery	PA
"	28		Visited Lines HQrs Horse Lines RA RE & Signals. DTVS. & Army (Col Larum) inspected 255 Bee RFA in afternoon — confirmed re diagnosis & CRA, arrangements Visited DTVs HQ Horse Lines RA RE Signals. Visited & inspected by RE in Line 30?	PP.
"	29		Visited & inspected H.Q.F. animals 532 L.K.C. Visited to VS. examined acc uncertain sporn cases. Ordered the evacuation. Visited & inspected 13 Squads no susp mange cases (one lad dress) hair evacuated. Inspected 14 Squadron 1 Pony horse temp temp 67 nil. Sent to Works for evacuation 1/ Attack on R.E. 1 susp mange sent to R.V.S. for evacuation. Inspected Horses HQ Bde. Bde Am. Tractor Pk Fort Tractor 1st HQr 1629 RF all healthy Trip 2 of Squadron 1 susp mange sent to RV.S. for evacuation. Received monthly deworming returns. Report distribution cups & to the dis- disinfection & isolation of animals in the infected units & received usages recurrently daily.	PP
			Colonel	

Army Form C. 2118.

WAR DIARY
or
INTELLIGENCE SUMMARY. 51st (H) Division
(Erase heading not required.)

Instructions regarding War Diaries and Intelligence Summaries are contained in F. S. Regs., Part II. and the Staff Manual respectively. Title pages will be prepared in manuscript.

April

Place	Date	Hour	Summary of Events and Information	Remarks and references to Appendices
Maroeuil	June 30th 1918	(Contd.)	Rates 404 Coy R.E. expected tomorrow, claimed all animals will be employed & 5 (3 Riders & 2 Supply horses) in transit area trades. Immediately examined all animals in 255 Res P.T.M. 1 Sup. horse from H.Q. Offr 255 Bde (slight wound) Private E.T.M.B. horse to No 3 O.Store line — R.E.'s disposals.	P.A.

P. Akers Major
A.D.V.S. 51st (H) Division

29 —   Vol 37

Confidential

War Diary
of 51st (H) Division
Sappers
for July 1918.

Army Form C. 2118.

WAR DIARY
of
INTELLIGENCE SUMMARY. 51=1(W) Division.
(Erase heading not required.)

Place	Date	Hour	Summary of Events and Information	Remarks and references to Appendices
Maricourt	July 1st		Tested Sr. WT lines lines, R&S + Signals. Tested + inspected 256 Bde R.P.S. + P.B.S. Wester lines + C+S reserves point. Signed 1 cam separater change lent to NWS for evacuation. Tested toupedoes no 1 Ex 57=6TTC. Wester fuin cam leap change + PWS. Inspected no 2 Ex 37=6TTC. evacuation port. A number of assaults in fire conduit set down for transit to base as surplus assaults including. Cap styles are + lay Eversman circ. &/c with surplus assaults to base. July 1st	
	2		Tested S&S W.O Gallins lines R.P.S. R&S Signals + Tested W.S. R.U.T. + recovered all recoverable at 253 Bac R.T.A. R.B.4. 2 Sup change to H.V.S.P. 3 Sups to large EWS. "C" + 4 Lanyard PAS. to 1 cam groepster new HQ Ordmus lines RPS. R&S + Signals, 1 Bde tome frm No.60154 for evacuation fr Minister. Tested toupedoes 152=153 + 154 R&S.	17
	3		Bane. Tested R&S XVII Corps. Tested SM + recovered + place in way from en-aimer Fleuve, R&S R&S R&S tg R&S w R.S. signals. Tested SPR trails Tested S&S W&Avenue lines	P/P
	4		Recovered 50 aussies for large 5 to 4 Basehament Report, Patrol Report.	

A 5334 Wt W4573/M657. 750,000. 8-16. D. D. & L. Ltd. Forms/C.2118/13.

Army Form C. 2118.

WAR DIARY
or
INTELLIGENCE SUMMARY. 51st (H) Division

(Erase heading not required.)

Instructions regarding War Diaries and Intelligence Summaries are contained in F. S. Regs., Part II. and the Staff Manual respectively. Title pages will be prepared in manuscript.

Place	Date	Hour	Summary of Events and Information	Remarks and references to Appendices
Mericourt	1916 Sept 4th contd		[illegible handwritten entries]	P.A.
"	5			P.A.
"	6			P.A.
"	7			P.A.
"	8			

Army Form C. 2118.

WAR DIARY
or
INTELLIGENCE SUMMARY. 57 (A) Division

(Erase heading not required.)

Original

Instructions regarding War Diaries and Intelligence Summaries are contained in F. S. Regs., Part II. and the Staff Manual respectively. Title pages will be prepared in manuscript.

Place	Date	Hour	Summary of Events and Information	Remarks and references to Appendices
Warmed	1916 July 8		(Continued) animals & 12 wagons to join 6th Bn in 73 Bde. Visited 283rd Bde/RFA lines R.E. Haynes.	P.A.
"	" 9		Self Jn in I.S. P. arranged with D.C. Common of 157 Hdaq we Modo Bde gunnette inspected	P.A.
"	" 10		Modo transport 283 Bde/RFA all animals & transports. Case of Mange. Modo transport 258 Bde/RFA All in good order. Conference with B.Cs.	P.A.
"	" 11		C.H.G. two Bde moved to Bellacourt. The officers stayed at 2pm (2nd & 3rd Bdes). Visited 17 Can Div to I.S.	P.A.
"	" 12		Returned H.F. Havre. Lectured I.W.M.R.C. others to Enquette in July 15	P.A.
"	" 13		Bunter Div Batter XVII Corps 10 Div & took over from 17th during two days. Received orders to entrain at 12 noon for unknown destination.	P.A.
"	" 14		Bde O.C. Br Entrained at Bries not reached during journey 15	
"	" 15		Arrived 4:15 Noon Siven Sept 8:25 pm	P.A.
"	" 16		2 hours intervals for inspect	P.A.
"	" 17		Entrained at Inform at 1 am. Thence to Tillewicance (4.5 Belmondo) Turker to Organise Tr 6. 50721	P.A.

Continued

April

WAR DIARY
or
INTELLIGENCE SUMMARY. 37/2(W)Division

Army Form C. 2118.

Place	Date	Hour	Summary of Events and Information	Remarks and references to Appendices
	1918		continued	
Moussy	Sep 18		Moved to Moussy. Officers & men in relation arrived. MFS Lidhaus XVII Artillery arrived.	P.A.
"	19		Advance HQs opened up at Moussy; MFS reports moved on to Champillowick 72 (W) Field Amb.	P.A. P.A. P.A.
"	20		Visited MFS and MDS asking for instructions on Evacuations.	P.A.
"	21		Orders MFS T. advance to DO Who	Moved XVII Corps HA up interview with the Authorities D.O.S. at HQ. MFS to evacuate to SWG Evacuating Station. J CLAMGES.	P.A.
"	22		Posted 13 (W) Field Amb. Posted 253 Bde Moved by train arranged for field for MFS Bivouacked at MOUSSY; posted to HQ	P.A. P.A.
"	23		MFS Advance Dn HQ Opened	P.A. P.A. P.A.
"	24		Posted 255 + 1259 Bde RFA. 76 Animals Released 17 Animals Destroyed	P.A.
"	25		Posted 154 T Bty Bde MFS T Detachment. Experience with DOS. Posted on ADOS MMP 9 FCR motors.	P.A.
"	26		Visited MFS T Detachment. 13 (W) Field Amb. Supplied All horses sent down to ABD.	P.A.

continued

WAR DIARY or INTELLIGENCE SUMMARY

Army Form C. 2118.

(Erase heading not required.)

Place	Date	Hour	Summary of Events and Information	Remarks and references to Appendices
Mussy	1918 July 27		Visited M.S. Signals & Div. Div. Div. (accounts)	PA
"	28		Visited M.S. & Div. H.Q. (Pact Manoeuvres) + H.Q. Receiving Station Div train.	PA
			Moved to Rendeuil in force.	
"	29		Visited Div. MoO. MVS (moved to 31 animals to XXII Evacuating Station)	PA
			Visited ADVS at Mareuil an Dy.	
"	30		Visited animals on A.S. - Visited M.S. & Collecting Post. Visited	PA
			M.D.S.V. - re evacuation of animals.	
"	31		Visited watering troughs & Collecting Post. Visited Spring herd -	PA
			took re entraining of (Artillery) animals. Instructed P.W. MVS	
			to move to Prine on 2/8/16. + entrain at Corps on 3/8/16.	

P. Moir Major
D.A.D.V.S.
51st (H) Division

WR 38

Confidential
War Diary
of
Sappers, 51st (H) Division
for August. 1918.

Original

WAR DIARY
or
INTELLIGENCE SUMMARY.

Army Form C. 2118.

51st (H) Division

Instructions regarding War Diaries and Intelligence Summaries are contained in F.S. Regs., Part II. and the Staff Manual respectively. Title pages will be prepared in manuscript.

(Erase heading not required.)

Place	Date	Hour	Summary of Events and Information	Remarks and references to Appendices
Mervoy	1918 Aug 1		Into MDS at Champfleury. Bades Evening Station superintended the entraining of 255 Bde R.F.A.	P.H
"	" 2		Bis. HQ. entertained at Cuisy (Champagne) en route for Pernes.	P.H
"	" 3		En route for Pernes. 1 case cerb. in H.D. of Div. H.Q. (Lt. Brockton) went through.	P.H
Pernes	" 4		Arrived Pernes 5am. Locked troops at Pullers Chalet Office in Chateau Grounds.	P.H 24
Villers Chatel	" 5		MDS. arrived from Champfleury. 85 occupied Camps at Ecriennes & Cuisy. Bades MDS arranged for dance. Into the Field Amb at Eurobigneuse. Into 51st R.E. B.V. at Cambligneuse.	
"	" 6		Bades Bis. the Ottomans Lines Boys at Fullers Chalet. Into the 2 Cy. train at Aubigny. Accts. A.D.S. Taylors R.F.A 2000. Bades with A.D.V.S. 8th Corps (Col Brook) 255 & 256 R Bdes 10FA for inspection. Arrivals in two Cavalry Brigades.	
"	" 7		Received R.F.A 2000 to ADVS 8th Corps for horses coming bug. 1st (relayed by move) Into the Bu Bks Horse Lines Ttigo. Into transport to 4 Cy. train + 152nd Sept. Bde. arrivals in good condition. Then inspected 16 Gunner Syphiteria and 10 MRS.	P.H P.H
"	" 8		Into BDS. of Dr. Horse Lines. Into MRS. Into 255 R & 256 Bdes 12F.A. 12 cars of Gas poisons in B256 to evacuate. Conference with FO.6.	P.H

Embarked.

WAR DIARY or INTELLIGENCE SUMMARY

Army Form C. 2118.

57th M? Brigade

(Erase heading not required.)

Original

Instructions regarding War Diaries and Intelligence Summaries are contained in F. S. Regs, Part II. and the Staff Manual respectively. Title pages will be prepared in manuscript.

Place	Date	Hour	Summary of Events and Information	Remarks and references to Appendices
Gillem Aerodrome	1918		(Continued)	
			Visited Bn HQ 40 Bty. Visited Hanis Cripple & inspected armt of Acrmnt. Horses & horses. Renewed PFA area.	PA.
"	10		Visited Ord N.C.Os. Horse lines. Btys. Visited R.H.E. Canada & received Remarks upon Arch-Arch. Stunts. Other new Artillery	PA.
"	11		Visited Bn HQ D-?mi lines & Signals. Visited Rimpact 132nd Bty Bde. Accounts in good condition. Visited & inspected 40 & Full Bty R.E. general run circular.	PA.
"	12		Visited Bn HQ & Horse lines. Visited & inspected 153 Bty Bde. NaBro 1 p.m. Visited Y? Black Watch at Chateau de la Haie. Several Pow generals Ord in for only poor fields. "D" Orden Stud at Bois de la Haie. Several NM arrivals. 1 Sanskrit	PA.
			1/2 Black Watch at Bois de la Haie. Several NM Arrivals. 1 Sanskrit Field of Magnifica term. Seradin not taggro. Practice. 1 Banner. Visited 400 Butt Bty R.E. 1 File wound 14 Riders under establishment	
"	13		Visited Bn HQ D-Horse lines Btys & RE's. Visited 255" & 258 Bde RFA. Low Full Bty	PA.
			TMB. 10 Btys XXII Corps (Col Munro) all arrivals inferior	
"	14		Visited Bn HQ & Horse Lines Btys & RE's h.V.S. instructed be b move to LARESSET before over from 57th Dint MB. Conference with JOC.	PA.
			Continued	

WAR DIARY or INTELLIGENCE SUMMARY

Army Form C. 2118.

572 (W) Division

Place	Date	Hour	Summary of Events and Information	Remarks and references to Appendices
Hilles Oaks	July 15		Visited Div HQ Problems Lines. Visited 159th Apy Bde. Pages to Stores at Capelon	P.A.
"	" 16		Visited Div HQ W Horse Lines + Pigs. HQ Office awaits DAD moved to MORBEUIL	P.A.
MORBEUIL	" 19		Visited Div HQ W Horse lines + Pigs. Visited XIII Corps MMP at Bernair Intam	
			with ADTS (Col Lake) Visited 57 Robs MRS at LARESSET arranged PM (W) M/S Reams)	P.A.
			HQPS 57 R's enclosed	
	" 18		Visited Div HQ W Horse Lines + Pigs. Rode to Marvent visited Knaptet 400 172	
			Section 57 DAC (Creator of Accounts fair) Visited Knaptet 73 (W) Field Amb	
			arrived in Army for evadition. MHS arrived at LARESSET. Reported same	
			arrivals in Army for evadition. Inspected 404 Field Cay RE. Animals & transport	P.A.
	" 19		to ADS XVII Corps. Inspected 404 Field Cay RE. Animals (Remarkable	
			Visited Div HQ W Horse Lines + Pigs (arrangements & work for Pigs in Baircheck	
			Visited SAA Section 572 DAC. Animals in good condition. Visited 255th + 256	
			Bde RFA at Madgascar Camps. Visited 152 A.P. Sec	P.A.
	" 20		Visited Div HQ Horse Lines + Pigs TMMP. Visited MHS + SAA Section)	P.A.
	" 21		Visited Div HQ W Horse Lines RH's IRE's + MMP. Visited 255th + 256th Bdes RFA	P.A.
			7/2 (W) Field Amb. 400 + 40 4 Field Coys at Loscoing at Lovay (Horse Commands)	P.A.
	" 22		Visited Div HQ W Horse Lines + Pigs, RE's RFA's. Conference w all rots.	P.A.
			Capts Anger, Norton, Roe + Lucking attended	

Continued

WAR DIARY or INTELLIGENCE SUMMARY

Army Form C. 2118.

57th A. Brigade

(Erase heading not required.)

Place	Date	Hour	Summary of Events and Information	Remarks and references to Appendices
MOREUIL	1916 Aug 23		Continued: 57(H) Brigade under command of Canadian Corps from 12 noon. Visited B.S.D.W.	P.A.
"	Aug 24		Horse lines R.A.s. R.E.s. Legs. 57th MMP. Visited 57 HD Ordnance Stores R.A.s. R.E.s. Legs. Visited M.I.C. + P/L Payne Section Staynover.	P.A.
"	25		Visited 57 HD Q. Hamilton. L.H.s. R.E.s. Legs. Visited H.Q. 363 Boy B.S.O. Visited M.I.C. Visited N.S. 363 Boy B.S.O. Inspected apartments at ECOIRES. Capt. Donnelly returned from leave. Arrived Terins Aug 25th.	P.A.
"	26		Visited Bos HD Ordnance lines R.A.s R.E.s Legs. Visited M.I.S. Heavily Shelled day & night	P.A.
"	27		Visited HQ Dr Horse lines R.Es + Legs. Visited 184th Labor. The Ypres area.	P.A.
Freking Camp	28		Moved to Freking Camp ECURIE. Visited B/23 HD Ordnance lines R.A. R.E. + Legs. R.A. R.E. + Legs. Visited 183 Atty Lee (commence to formation). Visited 401 Field Co. 255 Bde R.F.A. & 2 Lee Btts 57 Bde.	P.A.
"	29		Visited Bn HQ. Dr Horse lines R.A.s R.E.s + Legs. Visited 255 A.+255 Bdes R.F.A.	P.A.
"	30		S.S. No 2 Labor DAC. Conference with DOs. Visited HQ HD Horse lines R.A.s R.E.s + Legs. Visited 1 W Field Amb. 153rd Inf. Bde. 255 Bde R.F.A. Visited 187th Brd R.F.A. Inspected R.F.A. Boots.	P.A.

Continued.

Original

Army Form C. 2118.

WAR DIARY
or
INTELLIGENCE SUMMARY.   57th (W) Divn ADVS

(Erase heading not required.)

Instructions regarding War Diaries and Intelligence Summaries are contained in F. S. Regs., Part II. and the Staff Manual respectively. Title pages will be prepared in manuscript.

Place	Date	Hour	Summary of Events and Information	Remarks and references to Appendices
	1918			
Victory Camp	Aug 31		Visited Bgd HQ Or Hosp Divn RHs Rts & Hqs. Visited MVS. Visited XXII Corps 10.00 interviewed with DDVS. Visited 255 Bn RH at Dieppenaux assumed in for remainder	pp.
			P. Oken, Major DADVS. 51st (Highland) Division	

D.A.D.V.S.
51ST
(HIGHLAND) DIVISION
No.
28 SEP 1918

Confidential

War Diary

of 51st (H) Division

A.D.M.S. for

September 1918

WAR DIARY
INTELLIGENCE SUMMARY

Army Form C. 2118.

57th (Highland) Division

Place	Date	Hour	Summary of Events and Information	Remarks and references to Appendices
Maroeuil	1918 Sept 1		Visited Div HQ Dr Home Lines. RA & RE's T/grals. Visited 255 & 256 Bdes RFA. (Capt Bromley RFC reports Left Armstrong guts of my Battery etc. Applied to RAC base Depots for Sig'l NCO. T/phone Lieut Somerwer h 2 Co DHQ. Visited 401 Field Coy R.E. h.o 1 Co DHQ. 255 & 256 Bdes RFA. Musketry Valley. Visited in HQ D's Home Lines RAs RE's T/signals. Rode to 1 de DHQ several (illegible)	P.A.
"	2			P.A.
"	3		Visited Div HQ D Home Lines. PA RE's T/signals. Visited NHS. Visited "C" 255 A/Bde	P.A.
"	4		Visited Div HQ D Home Lines & CqS. 152nd Infy Bde. 153 -- Infy Bde. S-101 R.E.Par (Several Thro animals) h. 1 Coy Div Train (animals in good condition.) Visited C"75 - 255 Bde 77 3 Co DHQ	P.A.
"	5		Visited Div HQ D's Home Lines. RAs. RE's T/signals. (several units) Div Train BOYS 1st Army Postal h.F. 111 1 to Bigamaker I.T. Visited Div HQ Dr Home Lines + S'gnals ('C' case and C.BE); Visited Mills	I.T.
"	6		BOYs 22nd Corps. Visited s-101 Div D.E.Br (several Thro animals at 7Days) Visited Div HQ Drs Home Lines RAs RE's T/signals. Visited 153rd Infy Bde (Rocklingcourt)	P.A.
"	7		St Nicholas. Visited CHQ495 525 Div h S Coy at (Rocklingcourt Valley) all continued	P.A.

WAR DIARY
INTELLIGENCE SUMMARY

Army Form C. 2118.

37th W. Division

Place	Date	Hour	Summary of Events and Information	Remarks and references to Appendices
History Camp Beuvre	1916 Sep 7	cont	bespoke "O"; No SE 2858 P/A/Aug10thD.C.arf. asphalted for No 2 Veterinary Hospital (on duty with 1 & 2 sections at METZ) 4/90	P.H.
"	8		Visited Dr. Hd. Qr. Horse Lines R.H. R.E. & H. Signals (horses) Visited 161 FAs 2 section SMC (Capt. Havens & Capt. Angus. Calves)	P.H.
"	9		Visited Div. Hd. Qr. Horse Lines. R.E. & Signals. Visited 256 Bde RFA at Mordeby Valley (animals in good condition)	P.H.
"	10		Visited Div. HQ Qr. Horse Lines R.H. R.E. R.E.6 & Signals (Horse-lines outages for Calvalry) 256 Bde RFA. Visited (H) Field Ambulance (animals in good condition)	P.H.
"	11		Visited Div. HQ Qr. Horse Lines. R.E. & Signals. Visited 266 Bde RFA at 1st Ammunition	P.H.
"	12		City "D" General Horse Lines. Visited H.Q.S. Visited Div HQ Qr. Horse Lines R.E. & Signals Visited "A" B 256 Bde RFA General Horse animals on rest Battery	P.H.
"	13		Capples on 14th to relieve the 1st USA MVS (49th Division) Conference with HQS Visited Dir. HQ Qr. Horse Lines. 153 Bty Bde Div HQ P.F.A. Div Cav. & A.D.V.	P.H.
"	14		XVII Corps. Visited Div HQ Qr. Horse Lines Div Hd. Qrs. moved to Marevil Div Office Qrs. near Hourng MVS moved to Agnien (Continued)	P.H.

WAR DIARY
INTELLIGENCE SUMMARY.

Army Form C. 2118.

51st (H) Division

Place	Date	Hour	Summary of Events and Information	Remarks and references to Appendices
Bouquemaison	1918 Sept 15		Visited Div. HQ & Horse Lines R.E. & Signals. Visited M.V.S. The 3 Div. DAPS.	PA
"	" 16		" " " H.Q. Signals. Visited Bray Temporary Camp for M.V.S.	PA
"	" 17		Inspected M.V.S. & move to Bray. Visited to H.Q. Horse Lines R.E's & Signals. Visited 255 Bde R.H.A. all Regs (animals only in fair condition. D Bty goods, 5"Rein"; "A"/2 thin; "B" 306 C/10 thin. Visited 256 Bde R.H.A. all Regs. "A" Bty only fair, "B" not good. "C" Condition good, "D" fair; moved on due direction. Visited M.V.S.	PA
"	18		Same move to Bray. Visited M.V.S. Div. HQ Div. Horse Lines R.E's & Signals	PA
"	19		Visited Div. HQ Div. Horse Lines. R.E's. Signals & M.V.S. 172, 2 Bde 51 D.A.C. (animals in fair condition, strongly opposed; entry body, not equipment complete. Visited S.A.A. Section animals in fair condition. Conference with DDVS.	PA
"	20		Visited Div. HQ Div. Horse Lines R.E's & Signals. Visited M.V.S. operation bade for Equine.	PA
"	21		Visited DAPS. Div. HQ Div. Horse Lines. R.E & Signals. Visited Field Cashier.	PA
"	22		Visited M.V.S. Div. HQ Orthopaedic R.E & Signals. Visited 3rd D.A.C. (pm)	PA

Continued

Army Form C. 2118.

WAR DIARY
or
INTELLIGENCE SUMMARY. 37-(W) Divnr
(Erase heading not required.)

Place	Date	Hour	Summary of Events and Information	Remarks and references to Appendices
Maroeuil	Sep 22 (cont)		Ordered 255 R.F.A. + 258 R.F.A. Brigade A.D.T.S. 22nd Corps. Bridis M.C. on W.O. & Horse Lines Thynes. Proceed to the P. Horse Lines & H.Q.	P.A. P.A.
"	23		" Ordered ADVS 22nd Corps re report	
"	24		" Wrote to 255th Bde R.F.A. Bridis 258 Bde at day re animal inspect. Categories standard core in "A"B"+"C" Batteries. 2 of which were recommend. form'd no Course contain'd frequency newscase taken. Reported Remount at No 2 Coy Div train (not in possession) to intpt/Echelon but of carry'd of Remount for Artillery until Reg Id arrived at their Brigades for instruction. Proceeded to V.O. or Horse Lines R.H. Res Thynes.	P.A.
"	25		Camp Ecurie. Ordered 255 Bde R.F.A. 1 case of "B" strong andul Loans of standard. a remount that arrived Sep 23 from No 4. Remount Depot Reports same to ADVS XVII Corps. Ploughshares. to D.R.O. Ordered Hay Major RA reports name to him A/VS/mind 6 BRAY. P.A. Bridis ADO Horse Lines Battery. Bridis 255 Bde R.F.A. 2 men standard continued	P.A.
Achicy Camp Ecurie.	26			

WAR DIARY / INTELLIGENCE SUMMARY

Army Form C. 2118.

51st M/V Brown

Place	Date	Hour	Summary of Events and Information	Remarks and references to Appendices
Dieskau Camp	1918 26 Sep		Stromeliks in "C" 255 Bde. Visits M/S. 76 & 1/7 Black Watch Visits to the Ord Vom Lines. Visits 255 Bde RFA.	P.A.
"	27		Camp Levies. Visits Inspecto No 1 Sec 51 BAC. M/V moved to Balmoral. Visits 268 Bde RFA.	P.A.
"	28		a) Monthly Today (arrivals in preservation). Received AF A2000. Visits ADS. Visits 13 RE. 255 Bde RFA. C Bty 255 Bde RFA. C Bty 3 front lines Stromeliks. B) Mule evacuees. Visit 76 & 1/7 Black Watch with Cpt Ang & OC. 1 case Stromeliks 76 Bristol 2 in 1/7 Black Watch reported to ADVS. Visits to Royal Scots animals in preservation. Visits 150 M/Fft Bde & notified to Ord Own of Stromeliks.	P.A.
"	29		Sentences. Sent Report on Cpt Connelly to CRA 51st Division. Contacted with Pottinen lines & M.O.S. & Stromeliks cases in 255 Bde Visits	P.A.
"	30		102 & 103 MGB. arrivals in preservation. Visits to the Ord Vom lines & Regts. Visit & Inspect 256 Res RFA and Stromeliks. Visits DADS & Stromeliks cases (255 Bde 10 cases 76 B. Watch 1 case 1/7 2 cases)	P.A.

P. Afton Major AVC
DADVS 51st (Highland) Division

No 41

2A

Confidential
War Diary
of
51st. (H) Division
"A. & Q." to
October, 1918.

Army Form C. 2118.

WAR DIARY
or
INTELLIGENCE SUMMARY.   51st (Highland) Division
(Erase heading not required.)

Instructions regarding War Diaries and Intelligence Summaries are contained in F. S. Regs., Part II. and the Staff Manual respectively. Title pages will be prepared in manuscript.

Place	Date	Hour	Summary of Events and Information	Remarks and references to Appendices
Vieksy Camp Bouch	1918 Feb 1		Visited Div HQ. Ar Horse Lines & Mules; Visited Homable trees at Intelligence with RAOC's 1st Army (Col Reynolds) & 1st AVO's XVII Corps (Col Mason). First cases "B" 256 Bat/1H 3; C" 256 Bat 2. Total number of cases affects 18. Visited 16 Black Watch. Capt Mason's ave, cited.	P.A
"	2		Visited Div HQ Ar Horse Lines, RE's, RA's, Flagade. Visited 256 Bde P.H. Inspects all animals 9 cases Homable in S 735 755 all pneumonia. Visited HVS.	P.A
"	3		This effect moved from Methey Camp to Chateau D'Aigs. Visited HVS. HVS moved to BRAY; Visited RAOC's XVII Corps. received instruction from Col Mason to give assistance in administration of Corps Vin allocated during his absence on leave & in case of my moving out of the area to hand over to 1st HQPS 49th Division. Issued 51st Div Ham. Arranged HVS, Brice with Town Mayr. 6th owner: Visited ROVS. 1st Army for instructions as to disposal of Homable cases of 51st (H) Div. Continued	P.A

WAR DIARY
INTELLIGENCE SUMMARY

Army Form C. 2118.

57th (W) Division

Place	Date	Hour	Summary of Events and Information	Remarks and references to Appendices
Victory Camp	1918 Oct 4th		Continued	PA
Chatrice Camp	"4"		GOC's reported Road to works repaired at 11:30. GOC 14th Corps accompanied by Major B Capt H Bromley GSO to A' sector 11 a.m. 2:30 p.m. GOC's visited 1st Corps encountering Field units Brunette areas and SBMF (Capt Angus ford F.A.) in charge Major RE Instruction w/ course of Army by order the anzi-aircraft Brunety Stations. If 4 persons by 4 and Ray would travel with the Americans were entered. Enclosed at A.P.H. same visited the HQ of three Lines. A.E.'s & Corps 110 Div Director 401 Field Coy R.E. respecting dispute flies with case from D. coy, enclosed A.O. 15 Contalds Corridor culvert from D. 255 Pole mine from Traoling avenue R.O. with A.P. III. of July officer Quoted to 14th, 206/38, W. Alice Dee Brea (not occupied) Ceremonies 5 R.M.S. 110 officer preparing Rest etc continued	PA
	"5"			PA

WAR DIARY

Army Form C. 2118.

INTELLIGENCE SUMMARY

57th (W) Division

(Erase heading not required.)

Place	Date	Hour	Summary of Events and Information	Remarks and references to Appendices
Chateau d'Orp	Oct 6		Wrote Div. HQ Ops Horse lines stage 40th Field Coy R.E. examined 2 dugouts to Bernatre cave. Raided Corps HQ Dr TMKS. Decree to move on the 18th instant. MKS notified	P4. P4.
	7		Visited 2nd, 3rd, Bns Horse Lines, Corps HQ Or TMKS	
	8		Visited 2nd, 3rd, Bns Horse Lines, Corps HQ Or TMKS, Ors y MKS Line. Instructs MKS to move to Quéant on Oct 9th	P4.
Quéant	9		Visited 2nd 3rd Ors Horse Lines, Ors Offrs moved with Division. No Quarry Quéant. MKS moved to Quéant	P4.
Bourlon	10		Visited 2nd, 3rd Ors Horse Lines. moved to Chateau at Bourlon. MKS move to Ruby Jerouville, Bn H a 8-8.	P4.
Escaudoeuvres	11		Visited Bns TD Ors Horse Lines TMKS. Wrote B3 Inf Bde. Wrote 255 Bde RFA. Capt Taylor sick sent on leave 13th to 27th Oct. Lce/ New address Hawtrey's Horse Sackville, Lancashire. Cap Hawtrey called. Bn HQ Div. moved to Escaudoeuvres, MKS moved to trenches.	P4.

C.O. Ammed

WAR DIARY
or
INTELLIGENCE SUMMARY.

Army Form C. 2118.

(Erase heading not required.)

51st (W)Division

Place	Date	Hour	Summary of Events and Information	Remarks and references to Appendices
ESCAUDOEUVRES	7.4.18		(Continued)	
	12		Bntn H.Q. & Bn H.Q. Ors Move Rinds moved to NAVES	P.A.
	13		Bn H.Q. & Bn Ors Move Line & M.H.S. Ptn on Moving of Division.	P.A.
NAVES	14		Bn & Bngde Orders line R.E's R.H's R.H.Qs. Orders issued & Ptn at R.H. H.Qrs by Intercom with 5th division finalised by Confidence codes. X.X.H. V.5. S'	P.A.
"			moved to Centra. Capt Donnelly O/C. did not attend conference as instructed by wire.	P.A.
"	15		Orders Bns RH RES RHQs & Bns to Brigade cmmro & MCs	P.A.
"	16		M.H.S. moved to TULY Road near Railway embankment. Orders to Bns & Bns since 7.49 issued Ref post conference with Bns (Capt Donnelly not present)	P.A.
"	17		Orders Ins to H.O Dr Move Line R.H's 7 R.E.S. Rnte 255 Bruil RHQ. attends to Jur Orders. Received AT R.O.S.C Orders to HD Dr Move Rite 5 Bn H.S.Bn 7.23 RES RHQ.	P.A.
"	18		Orders Corps Headquarters	P.A.
			(Continued)	

WAR DIARY
or
INTELLIGENCE SUMMARY

Army Form C. 2118.

57-(W) Division

(Erase heading not required.)

Place	Date	Hour	Summary of Events and Information	Remarks and references to Appendices
	1918		continued	
NAVES	19/19		Visited Bns. H.Q. Ordnance. Divn. CRAs RE & Signals. Divn'l MHS.	P.A.
"	20		" " " " " " Div HQ Ordered to AVESNE	P.A.
THUN ST MARTIN	21		Divn. Offices moved to THUN ST MARTIN joining HQ/MHS; 257.S. 1st Army (N'col Ruvd) inspected MHS.	P.A.
"	22		Visited Bns. HQ O. Horse Lines RAs REs & Signals at Avesne le sec Pavé de VALENCIENNE.	P.A.
"	23		Divn Offices + MHS. moved to Pavé de VALENCIENNE. Visited Bns 1 + 2 Bns Divl Train. Visited Bns HQ O. advanced to see CRAs RA REs & Sigs. RA RE & Sigs.	P.A.
PAVÉ de VALENCIENNES	24		Moved Bn. H.Q. Ordnance bivis RA RE & Sigs. 1 Bivisite DOUCHY H.Q.d + two Field Coy R.E. 256 Bde. R.F.A. 7th Bde R.F.A. Visited NOYELLE	P.A.
"	25		Visited Bn HQ Ordnance. Divs. Telegraphs. Bivisite trips to HQ Ws.	P.A.
"	26		Visited Bn HQs. Horse Lines RA RE REs & Signals. Bivisited Douchy (Copy attacked.) See information send 206	P.A.
"	27		Bivisite Bns. off HQ. RA & H RH GaphamesiH will 20d appearance Order completed continued	

WAR DIARY
or
INTELLIGENCE SUMMARY.

Army Form C. 2118.

(Erase heading not required.)

51st (H) Division

Place	Date	Hour	Summary of Events and Information	Remarks and references to Appendices
VALENCIENNES	1918 Oct 27		Continued.. in my absence reports to Div General to recommend Two orderlys: Orders 405 Field Coy RE Donnely (civilian school teacher) Brest at Ront	P.H.
	28		Orders Donnely promoted Capt. Receives MC. Stems German counter order. Thought of Noyelle desperately	P.H.
	29		Orders to 407 Br. Horse Ambu RHS Rks. Hdqs at Avesnes. Orders to 405 field coys + Br. E. Br. of Donnely + Hypotte Mater Royal Scots + 407 Br. Horse Amb RHS RFC Roquale . Orders RHs Orderes	P.H.
	30		Orders 405 Rks. Horse ambu RHs Roquala . visits R.ACs Orferes will pros, Capt Donnelly 2nd Lieut Orientat 2nd SWB Rks. Home Ambu RHs Roquair . vers 1st Army CCd	P.H.
	31		This offnr moved to Ivory : MS moved to Boger factory Ivory: Capt Taylor returns from leave	P.H.

P. Altson Major
11.11.18 57th (Highland) Division

D.A.D.V.S.
51st
HIGHLAND DIVISION
26 - 3 NOV 1918

WO 4 2

Confidential

War Diary

of

D.A.D.V.S. 51st (H) Div.

for

November 1918

Army Form C. 2118.

WAR DIARY
or
INTELLIGENCE SUMMARY. 57²/(W) Bngoo.

(Erase heading not required.)

Instructions regarding War Diaries and Intelligence Summaries are contained in F. S. Regs., Part II. and the Staff Manual respectively. Title pages will be prepared in manuscript.

Place	Date	Hour	Summary of Events and Information	Remarks and references to Appendices
Izvay	Nov 1 1918		Visited Pigs H.Q. Or Horse Lines R.B's Flights. Visited N.S. T.57 & B. A.S	PP
"	2		Br at Parliament. (Revised Xmas Accounts.)	
"	3		Visited B5 SQ Q. Horse Lines R.B's Flights V.A.M.S. Visited No 2 Coy 57st	PP
"			R.S. Train at 7 by El Park (Moving) inspected Remount	
"	4		Visited Pigs H.Q. Or Horse Lines R.B's Flights. Visited N.S. Received line	PP
"			from O/C 18/255 R Sqie R.A.F. notifying death of Lieut A.R Barker and	
"			Visited B5 SQ Q. Horse Lines R.B.S. Flights. Visited N.S. Visited 5/17 A.S	
"			B A. Parliament H.Q. Accounts in September. B. H.C not good	
"			several the animals showing not poor. Capt Ayler O/C went	
"	5		on leave. Lieut Taylor Q/O supposed to take command B h/(W) A.S	PP
"			Visited CE B5 Q. Horse Lines R.A.F. Flights. Paid to Expenses for Rations	
"			Office Manis.	
"	6		Visited No H.Q. Or Horse Lines R.G. Flgs. Visited N.S. Capt Ayler leave	PP
"			now at R.D??	
"	7		Visited Bn. No Or Horse Lines R.A.S. Flgms . Visited N.S. inspected A.A 2 pers	PP
"	8		Visited Bn No Or Horse Lines R.B.S. Flights. Visited N.S.	

A.R.Turner

WAR DIARY
INTELLIGENCE SUMMARY.
(Erase heading not required.)

Army Form C. 2118.

Place	Date	Hour	Summary of Events and Information	Remarks and references to Appendices
Savy	1918 Nov 8		Continued	
			R.S. moved to 10th F.S.D. Camp at Savy. Received Capt. Donnelly's instructions to O.C. Mine G.H.C. detailed as escort to Remenfer	P.P.
	9		Remenfer 10 O.R. to Mine line R&S returns. N.S.	P.P.
	10		Routine 10 O.R. Mine line R&S Repair & Routes then Commenced	M.
	11		Survey repairs for O.C. Mines. Routine. 10 O.R. Sustain line. R&S Repair. Printed M.S. Direction Copied to take effect from Noon	P.P.
	12		Routine 10 O.R. Sustain line. R&S Repair at Artillery L/Cpl Wootton R.E. Mar Gurney. Printed 152 copy. Rue de Theinne St Martin judgments Clearing Important all delivery came in for exhibition	P.P. P.P.
	13		[illegible] 10 to Horse line R&S Repair Routes R.E	P.P.
	14		Routine 10 O.R. 10 Horse line R&S Repair Routes Area Commanders	P.P.
	15		Printed M.S.	P.P.
	15.		Routine 10 O.R. 10 Horse line R&S Repair Routes held for [illegible]	P.P.
			Arrivals at Signals. Same in progress also	P.P.
	16		Routine 10 O.R. Horse line R&S & Reports. Printed M.S. Commenced at Paper Sketch Survey	P.P.
				Continued

Army Form C. 2118.

WAR DIARY
or
INTELLIGENCE SUMMARY.   51st (H) Division

(Erase heading not required.)

Place	Date	Hour	Summary of Events and Information	Remarks and references to Appendices
Torcy [?]	1918 July 17		Continued. W.O. to 2 i/c & Hors. Lines Kts & Signals &. 2i/c to 153 Inf Bty Bde Hrs wef to 5 march. 2i/c to R.H.S. 2i/c to 2/c & 2/c Hr sub instruments.	PH
	18		Wrote 256 Bde R.F.A. at Harangeres (Mens and inspects all animals. Same "B" 3 Replace. "B" 3 Replace. "B" 3 Replace "B" 3 Replace to 4 Replace "B" 2 Replace for "C" consideration. "B" 3 Replace to 253 Bde R.F.A. at Grony Belfron, animals in fair condition, "A" Bty "B". 3 Replace, "C". 2 Replace, "D". 4 Replace. "D" of Replace (Sphalerne). Around fatre J 307pm.	PH
	19		Orders Dir W Dn. Hose Lines R86 Replace. In to W.S inspected animals. Returned Served animals which were Newcomer came for over exam. Returned "O"n the matter.	PH
	20		Wrote SN NO ambulances units, R86 Flys, wrote N.Y.C. wrote 252 aux Horse Transport Co at Trony, animals in good condition. Conference with ROC.	PH
	21		Wrote 6x No Q & Horse Lines R8C Signals Wrote to 154 R.H.y Bde 21 (H) Field Ambulance, 404 Field Coy R.B., No 2 Coy Div Train. Animals all satisfactory.	PH

Continued.

Army Form C. 2118.

WAR DIARY
or
INTELLIGENCE SUMMARY
(Erase heading not required.)

51st N Div — ?

Place	Date	Hour	Summary of Events and Information	Remarks and references to Appendices
Itzay	1918 Nov 22		Wrote to O.s.T.D. Orthena Sigs. R.B.S. & Signals: Wired M.D.S.: Wired 154th Fd. Amb. at Hq. 51st Div... G.O.C. 51st Div inspected Dump. Several cases of chippery received against evacuations. Informed Col. Davidson D.A.D.V.S. re Cov to meet A.T.C. A 2912. Wired... met Capt. Taylor.	P.A.
	23		Wrote 51st M.M.d Blanques (Belgians) inspected No 1 & 2 Sections. Arrivals in Fair condition. Wired re evacuation of horses & sickly from No 2 Section. Wired to No 22 V.E.S. (arrives back with car 7-35)	
	24		Capt. Angar returned from leave. Wrote A.D.V.S. Arthorne Lines. R & T Lys.	P.T. P.A.
	25		Wrote Lis. A.D.V.S. Arthorne Lines. R & T Lys. Wrote M.D.S. Wrote S.A.H. Icehm.	P.A.
	26		Wrote Lis. A.D.V.S. Arthorne Lines. R & T Lys. Wrote V.E.S. Aberdaron t Bordeaux. Wrote 1/6 Royal Scots.	P.A.
			"	
	27		At Edwin with Capt. Angar are arrived in pm Convoies. Wrote A.D.V.S. Arthorne Lines. R.B.c. Signals: Wired R.E.S.	P.T. P.A.
	28		Wrote Ets. N.O Arthorne Lines R.B.S. Signals (Wired of this week in afternoon)	P.A. P.T.
	29		"	P.T. P.A.
	30		Wrote in afternoon 6 in afternoon	

N. Abram Major
A.D.V.S. 51st (H) Division

War Diary
A.D.M.S. 51st (H) Division
Dec 31st 1918.

D.A.D.V.S.
51st
(HIGHLAND DIV...)
No. 1303
Date 3.1.1914

Army Form C. 2118.

WAR DIARY
or
INTELLIGENCE SUMMARY. 57th (W) Division
(Erase heading not required.)

Instructions regarding War Diaries and Intelligence Summaries are contained in F.S. Regs., Part II. and the Staff Manual respectively. Title pages will be prepared in manuscript.

Place	Date	Hour	Summary of Events and Information	Remarks and references to Appendices
TMUY	1918 Dec 1st		Visited Bde HQ O/Horse Lines, R.E.s, Telegraph TMVS	P.H.
"	" 2		"	P.H.
"	" 3		"	P.H.
"	" 4		Visited forward area; attended British pm OC, min horses etc / 1r AVS at Bouquemaison. Belgians; interviews with AQVS & DDVS Corps at home; Visited inspected 258 Bde RFA at Rouelle; animals in good condition.	P.H.
"	" 5		Visited & inspected animals of 255th Bde RFA at Rouelle; animals in good condition. Returned to TMUY by car.	P.H.
"	" 6		Visited Bde HQ O/Horse Lines, Signals TMVS; Visited 57th A.G.Br. & Cross Kempston Cops; Formerly RMVC	P.H.
"	" 7		Visited Bde HQ O/Horse Lines, Signals TMVS; arranged for treatment of mentaleme memories	P.H.
"	" 8		Visited Bde HQ O/Horse Lines, R.E.s Telegraph Signals; DDVS inspected horses of DHQ. ADV8 sanctioned clipping of 1 Rium & 3 CO. 57th Dr. & Br for heavy aims horses. 57th Dr. & Br wrote re instructions as to preventive measures	P.H.
"	" 9		Visited Bde HQ O/Horse Lines, R.E.s, Signals TMVS. Wrote No 3 Cy Train inspected to ascertain some truck	P.H.

CONTINUED

WAR DIARY (2)
INTELLIGENCE SUMMARY. 5/-1 (W) Division

Army Form C. 2118.

Place	Date	Hour	Summary of Events and Information	Remarks and references to Appendices
ENVY	Dec 10		Continued	
			This officer moved to No 22 Bull. Imp.; Instructed Capt J.F. Donnelly R.A.M.C. to report to War Office at once. Handed over to Capt Ayer R.A.M.C.; Capt Ayer instructs take over school equipment; handed No 21 Orderly Civil R.B. & Thos.	P.H.
			Went on leave to England (authority W.O. telegram A.D.M.S. XIII Corps Cat Homer 13 Dec F.27.) Handed over duties of Capt J.F. Ayer R.A.M.C. Capt L.F. Donnelly Capt for England. Handed over to O/C Y. (H) H.V.S. 1 details.	P.H.
"	11		(officer) + 1 officer visited out compete	P
"	12		Visited Bus. H.Q. O Horse Lines. R.E. Telephone Trans.	P.T.O.
"	13		Inspected Horse Lines of 153rd Bty. Bde. 72 (H) Field Amb. moved there	P.T.O.
"	14		Visited Horse Lines of 152nd Bty. Bde. Div. H.Q. O.r. Telegraph.	
"	15		Brakes on H.Q. O.r. Horse Lines. Permission granted to Sergt. 1 Co. cutting from Cure belonging to 153rd 2nd R.F.A.; Lieut Corps R.A.M.C. reports for duty. 1 other offence class + 1 officer walked handed to Camp. Receipt obtained	P.T.O. P.T.O.
"	16		Visited Horse Lines of 13 (H) Field Amb. + the Royal Corps; A.D.M.S. XIII Corps P.T.O. notified of arrival of Lieut Corps R.A.M.C.	P.T.O.

Continued

Army Form C. 2118.

WAR DIARY
or
INTELLIGENCE SUMMARY.
(Erase heading not required.)

51st (W) Division

Place	Date	Hour	Summary of Events and Information	Remarks and references to Appendices
INUY	1918 Dec 17		Visited Div HQ or Horse Lines, 51st M.S.B., 400 & 401 Field Coys R.E., 07 horses permission troops. 1 Rider in bee belonging to M.M.S.: Capt Y.S. in Cape R.M.O. reported for duty with 255th Bde R.F.A. at Roculx, Belgium. 1 Case stomatitis contagiosa, a recent reported in No 4 Coy A.S.C. by Capt Taylor R.A.V.C. Visited Horse Lines of 153rd Arty. Bde. & 154th Arty Bde Group with a view to treating purpose. A.D.V.S. Corps informed re outbreak	2.7.Q.
"	" 18		stomatitis in No 4 Coy A.S.C. & necessary precautions taken. Visited Horse lines of Div HQ Oro & 152nd Inf Bde Group for purpose of ascertaining means of averting purposes. Capt Warren took instructs	2.7.Q.
"	" 19		re outbreak of stomatitis in remount. Visited Horse Lines of Div HQ Oro Signals, 1/7 Black Watch (1 case stomatitis) & 1/6 Argyll Sutherland Highlanders & supply of hors noised to need to work. Visited Horse Lines of Div HQ Oro Signals. A.D.V.S. XXII Corps inspected	2.7.Q.
"	" 20			2.7.Q.
"	" 21		H.V.S. also stomatitis case at No 4 Coy Train & examined hors for treating purpose.	2.7.Q.
"	" 22		Visited Horse Lines of 153rd Inf. Bde. & 1/5 Leopolds: Permission Continued	2.7.Q.

WAR DIARY
INTELLIGENCE SUMMARY.   51st (W) Division

Army Form C. 2118.

Place	Date	Hour	Summary of Events and Information	Remarks and references to Appendices
	1915		Continued	
INUY	Dec 22	cont	Paid to staff 3 & 8 Tamany & 2nd Bde R.F.A.	P.T.Q.
"	23		Visited Horse Lines of B & B Wr Signals; also 152nd Inf Bde; sent one to RAMC for huts that located here at H.W.	P.T.Q.
"	24		Visited Horse Lines of 57, 58 & 59, 400 & 401 Field Coys R.E.s, 1/3 (H) Field Amb, 1 River Aux from L.S.B. for examination	P.T.Q.
"	25		Visited Horse Lines of Div HQrs, Div Signals, 1/5 Seaforths, 1/6 Seaforths, No 3 Coy A.S.C. + 50 Motors ones at 2, 3 & 4 Coy A.S.C. to supply of harness to Div units	P.T.Q.
"	26		Visited Horse Lines of 152nd Inf Bde, 16 Seaforths, 1/3 (W) Field Amb; Pte Brogan, Clerk, went to town; Pte Birkwood took one stable; Motor Cars etc[?] went from RMS; Authority regrant to keep 1/25 Pte ties[?] belonging to 1/9 Black Watch	P.T.Q.
"	27		Visited Horse Lines of Div HQ Div Sigs & signals; land newly AFA given to ADVS.	P.T.Q.
"			1/6 Argylls etc.	
	28		Visited to Div Orthrs Lines Rlys (?H? absence of of also 1/6 + 1/7 Black Watch. Contained Dep, Arm to changes of commands for Demobilization road by C.W. to his own harness killed - 8 hrs.	P.T.Q.

Army Form C. 2118.

WAR DIARY
or
INTELLIGENCE SUMMARY. 51st (H) Division
(Erase heading not required.)

Place	Date	Hour	Summary of Events and Information	Remarks and references to Appendices
INVY	1918 Dec 29		Continued — Made arrangements for Billets & Stabling for H.Q. at new area. Visited 255th & 256th Bdes RFA at Roedloe. Interviewed Capt Warren.	P.P.B
"	30		Returned by car from new area. Major P. Khan returned from leave. Visited the base at H.Q. 2 Employment Coys 1 MVS	P.Q.
"	31		Took over duties of DADVS from Capt Angus RAVC Visited Divl Od Horse Lines. Signed thus	PH

P. Khan Major
DADVS 51st (Highland) Division

D.A.D.V.S.,
51st
(HIGHLAND) DIVISION.
No. 1302
Date 31-1-19

11/3

No 44

D.A.D.V.S.
51st
(HIGHLAND) DIVISION

War Diary.
D.A.D.V.S 51st (H) Division
for January 1919.

Army Form C. 2118.

WAR DIARY
or
INTELLIGENCE SUMMARY.
(Erase heading not required.)

57th (W) Division

Place	Date	Hour	Summary of Events and Information	Remarks and references to Appendices
INVY	1919 July 2		Conference with R.O.S. arranged for Road of eval. Officer & Veterinary Officer re. Boulogne animals. Parts M/S	
	3		Epidemic 15 Royal Scots, Veterinary board examined & Volunteered all animals reported for evacuation animals of H. (W) Field Amb 74 transit officers. Details the 7th Rifle & Rutherford. Ship transit. 1080/159 Rifle Bde to M/S. The 2nd K.S.L.I. & 57th W.div recover.	PH
	4		Visits M/S. Board on animals H. (W) M/S.	PH
	5		Board on animals of 510 W.A. 812 M.M.P.	PH
	6		Cond. inspect. 158th Inf. Bde. 4072 N4.MS & H.Auk. water, & father L & P. 521 Combined Regnl Police & Cavalry Detachment Hy Flanders.	PH
	7		Visits Detachm. 521 M.G.Bn. M.M.P.& 154 Inf. Bde. 404 Field Coy R.E.	PH
	8		H.W. visited city section road & bridges & trenches between stops & Avy	PH
	9		Visits Hosp. Event Ship Jemappes.	PH
	10		H.V.O. visited 2/A LOUVIERE (Belgium) the A.V.O. 300 & Hy 46 Field Amb. La Louviere.	PH
LA LOUVIERE	11		Visits Div. HQtrs Q. T. Bde Gy. t Arty	PH
	12		Visits Div. HQ Gen Horse Lines. Quartes Div. H.Q. Gen Horse lines, Transport arrived. Continued	PH

Original

Instructions regarding War Diaries and Intelligence Summaries are contained in F. S. Regs., Part II. and the Staff Manual respectively. Title pages will be prepared in manuscript.

WAR DIARY
or
INTELLIGENCE SUMMARY.
(Erase heading not required.)

51st (H) Division

Army Form C. 2118.

Place	Date	Hour	Summary of Events and Information	Remarks and references to Appendices
	1919		Continued.	
La Louvière	May 13		Board visited & inspected 152nd Inf Bde, 1/2 (H) Field Ambulance.	P.H.
"	14		" " " 400th Field Coy RE & 1/3rd (H) Field Ambulance	P.H.
"	15		Board visited & inspected No 3 Coy Train & part of 1st Coy & 401 Field Coy RE. [illegible] Office moved to Billet No 73 La Louvière.	P.H.
"	16		Board visited & inspected A & B Btys 256 Bde RFA.	P.H.
"	17		" " " C & D " " " Returns sent to ADVS xxii Corps	P.H.
"	18		" " " A & B Btys 255 Bde RFA & [illegible] 255 Bde RFA	P.H.
"	19		" " " B & C Btys 255 " "	P.H.
"	20		" " " Nos 1 & 2 Sections 51st DAC. Returns sent to ADVS	P.H.
"	21		" " " No 3 (SAA) Section & HQ 51st DAC	P.H.
"	22		" " " 10th & 97 Btys 147 Bde RFA } at Soignies	P.H.
"	23		" " " A & [illegible] Btys 147 Bde RFA }	P.H.
"	24		" " " 147 B.A.C. Returns sent to ADVS	P.H.
"	25		" " " No 4 Coy A.S.C. 51st Div Train.	P.H.
"	26		" " " No 1 Coy " at [illegible]	P.H.
"	27		General Routine Office work	P.H.

Continued

D. D. & L., London, E.C. (A8004) Wt. W1771/M2 31 750,000 5/17 Sch. 52 Forms/C2118/14

Army Form C. 2118.

WAR DIARY
or
INTELLIGENCE SUMMARY.

(Erase heading not required.)

April 51st (H) Divn

Place	Date	Hour	Summary of Events and Information	Remarks and references to Appendices
La Source Camp	28		R.T. Bound. Guards relieved. Part of No 1 Cy, R.S.C. Re-railed & 28 Legions decimals	PH
	29		General Routine. Reinforcements ord. to MPS. MT lorries Supplies tendered	PH
	30		Dr Sloop. Lr. RD Officers leave. General Routine	PH
	31		Reynolds. General Routine	PH

J Allen Major
DADVS 51st Highland Division

D.A.D.V.S.
51ST
(HIGHLAND) DIVISION.
No.
Date

Vol 45

9

D.A.D.V.S.
51st
(HIGHLAND) DIVISION
No. ....
Date. 4/3/19

War Diary.
D.A.D.V.S.
51st (H) Division.

Army Form C. 2118.

WAR DIARY
or
INTELLIGENCE SUMMARY. 51st (W) Divisional ...

(Erase heading not required.)

Instructions regarding War Diaries and Intelligence Summaries are contained in F. S. Regs., Part II. and the Staff Manual respectively. Title pages will be prepared in manuscript.

August

Place	Date	Hour	Summary of Events and Information	Remarks and references to Appendices
Cologne Hspt	1919		Wrote M.S. General Office Routine. Sent weekly returns to H.Q.'s XXII Corps	A
"	2		Wrote HQRS XXII Corps. General office routine	A
"	3		Wrote A.S. 401 Field Coy R.E. Some accounts in but credit in Experience with H.O.S. re returns	A
"	4		Wrote M.S. Conference with D.O.C. re charge of debility. General Routine	A
"	5		Wrote Divl. Artillery & related 2 accounts for sale. Wrote M.S.	A
"	6		Wrote M.S. & HQ.'s XXII Corps. Wrote 51st BHC collects accounts for Sale.	A
"	7		Wrote HQRS above Divis, Signals (M.V.S. Pro & Corp F.S.C.	A
"	8		Wrote HQRS To Sale & accounts at moon for instruction Expense	A
"	9		Gave Corp-off group (Col Kerr) Second Office Routine	A
"	10		Wrote M.V.S. General Office work. Compiled weekly return	A
"	11		Wrote M.V.S. Wrote HQRS XXII Corps	A
"	12		Wrote E.R.A. re Salvaging Artillery Animals for Sale. Sale To accounts from 256th Br.R.H. Also 1 & 2 TubDro 51st BHC	A
"	13		Wrote 401 Field Coy R.E. & 3 accounts for Sale & 3 from Store No O.R. Continued.	A

Army Form C. 2118.

WAR DIARY
or
INTELLIGENCE SUMMARY. 57th (W) Division

(Erase heading not required.)

Instructions regarding War Diaries and Intelligence
Summaries are contained in F.S. Regs., Part II.
and the Staff Manual respectively. Title pages
will be prepared in manuscript.

Place	Date	Hour	Summary of Events and Information	Remarks and references to Appendices
La Louvre	1919 Jul 14		Visited R.T.S.; Visited Achille Crozier, 7 Rue de la Gare to discuss arranged private	
"	15		9 arrivals on 1st C.F.	P.T.
"	16		Visited A.P.S.; Bn Signals Res + Or H.Q. go. Visited Corps with returns	P.T.
"	17		Visited 5p.p Horse Lignes. General Office Routine	P.T.
"			Held sale of 150 animals at Place Gambrinus. Led by Insp Crozier	
"			Total auctioned realized 135,500 fs. Paid to auctioneer 6,775 fs. Comm.	P.T.
"	18		at 5%. Handed Proceeds of Sale to Field Cashier	P.T.
"			Visited A.P.S. + Divisional Artillery; General Office Routine	
"	19		Visited 154th Bty. Bde. 140 O.R. Bde. 153 (H) Bty Bde. 201 + 202 Field Coy R.E.	P.T.
"	20		Selectors arrived for sale of horses; No 2 Rech. 17/18" selects animals for sale.	P.T.
"	21		Visited Hos Vale Coy, R.E. + No 2 Rech. 17/18" General Office Routine	P.T.
"	22		Visited A.D.V.S. Rendered weekly returns. Capt Warner R.M.C. returns	P.T.
"			Gen Hospital 13/15/08. Pte Scott L.O. 51 R.E. Bn reports for duty	
"	23		Visited Brig. H.Q.30r Horses	P.T. P.T.
"			General Routine. Visited Lines Agines.	

(Continued)

Original

WAR DIARY
or
INTELLIGENCE SUMMARY. 51st (H) Division

Army Form C. 2118.

Place	Date	Hour	Summary of Events and Information	Remarks and references to Appendices
La Louvie	7/8/19 24	Continued	Sale of 2 surplus animals at Kit Louvie. Aerond realize 1556.0.0 This sanctioned. 3.890 fe being 2/3 of commission paid with top field cashier.	P.H.
"	25		General office routine. Ended 670,740 Oro Arrivals. 7 signals.	P.H.
"	26.		General office routine. Instructed Capt Taylor R.A.V.C. to rebel mares for farmers in U.K.	P.H. P.H.
"	27		General office routine. On to 51st R.Q.B., 153 Inf. Bde. 12 & 21st Drifish Auxo. Depots.	P.H.
"	28		Compiled weekly return. Animals for sale:	P.H.

P. Hbson. Major. D.A.V.S.
51 (H) Division

D.A.D.V.S.
51st
HIGHLAND DIVISION

www.ingramcontent.com/pod-product-compliance
Lightning Source LLC
Chambersburg PA
CBHW081407160426
43193CB00013B/2124